cuddle me quick

11 BABY-QUILT DESIGNS

Christine Porter & Darra Williamson

Martingale
Create with Confidence

dedication

- ➤ To Darra's (younger) sisters, Loretta and Charlie, *still* the prettiest babies she has ever seen.
- ➤ And in loving memory of Chris's sister, Sally Ann.

ACKNOWLEDGMENTS

We'd like to thank the following for their support and generosity:

- ➣ The Cotton Patch, UK, for Cotty threads and fabric
- ➣ Midsomer Quilting, UK
- ➣ Husqvarna Viking, UK
- ➣ Our *fabulous* team at Martingale & Company
- ➣ Darra's "blogging sisters"—Christie Batterman, Laura Nownes, and Jennifer Rounds
- ➣ As always, our wonderful husbands, Neil Porter and Brooks Sheifer

MISSION STATEMENT
Dedicated to providing quality products and service to inspire creativity.

Cuddle Me Quick: 11 Baby-Quilt Designs
© 2012 by Christine Porter and Darra Williamson

Martingale®
19021 120th Ave. NE, Suite 102
Bothell, WA 98011 USA
ShopMartingale.com

Printed in China
17 16 15 14 13 12   8 7 6 5 4 3 2 1

Library of Congress Cataloging-in-Publication Data is available upon request.

ISBN: 978-1-60468-151-2

CREDITS

President & CEO: Tom Wierzbicki
Editor in Chief: Mary V. Green
Design Director: Paula Schlosser
Managing Editor: Karen Costello Soltys
Technical Editor: Ursula Reikes
Copy Editor: Marcy Heffernan
Production Manager: Regina Girard
Illustrator: Christine Erikson
Cover & Text Designer: Adrienne Smitke
Photographer: Brent Kane

contents

introduction

The world is changing *so quickly* around us; it seems that every day brings a new "something" that we must learn, adapt to, or do. One thing doesn't change, however, and that is the fact that sweet little babies are born every day.

A soft, cuddly quilt, scaled down to baby size, is a wonderful way to welcome a little one into the world. Over the years, we've both made many quilts for special babies and toddlers in our lives, Chris for her grandchildren, Darra for her nieces and nephews, both of us for the children (and grandchildren!) of friends. You'd think we would have come up with the idea for this book sooner! Yet it wasn't until Chris learned that two of her young friends were expanding their little family, and proceeded to make "Grace's Quilt" (page 41) for their newborn daughter, that our plan for creating a book of fresh, new designs for Baby began to take shape.

In the following pages, you'll find instructions for 11 small quilts. We aimed for a mix of reworked classic designs and originals created just for this book. Some are pieced, some are appliquéd, and some are a combination of both techniques. *All* are made using simple, straightforward techniques— rotary cutting; strip piecing and other timesaving methods; fusible, machine-finished appliqué—to make the construction easy, accurate, and fun.

Keeping in mind that many first quilts are made by expectant moms (and grandmoms and aunties), we've made sure to include projects of all skill levels. Many are *super simple,* perfect for beginners, while still rewarding and appealing enough to tempt the more experienced quilter. Others require a bit more experience, but our goal was to make the step-by-step instructions detailed enough, and the diagrams plentiful enough, that even a rookie has a good shot at success.

In addition to the project instructions, we've tucked a lot more info into these 80 pages! You'll find a healthy basics section with some of our favorite methods for things like adding triangles to squares or rectangles and applying sleeves and bindings. There are *dozens* of tips scattered throughout; some are project specific, while others address fundamentals that you can apply to *any* quilt. If a project is a good match for charm packets, precut strips, or fat quarters, we tell you so. And as for that generic "Quilt as desired"? Well, you can if you'd like, but if you're stumped for a plan, each project includes suggestions for quilting, thoughts about thread, and a nice, big photo of Chris's quilting on that particular project.

In short, we've tried to make the quiltmaking process as relaxing, easy, and enjoyable as possible. We hope you'll fall in love with one (or more!) of our little quilts, and use your hands, your heart, and your creativity to welcome *your* special little one into the world.

Fondly,

Chris & Darra

quiltmaking basics

▼▼

Here is where we give you lots of general information you'll need to make the little quilts in this book. While each project includes step-by-step instructions specific to that quilt, these pages include tips and techniques that apply to some or all of them. At times, you'll be referred to this section, and—we suspect—you may wander here on your own; in fact, you might want to bookmark these pages.

For more information about basic quiltmaking techniques, visit ShopMartingale.com/HowToQuilt. There you'll find information on how to appliqué, sew borders on a quilt, make a quilt sandwich, and common hand-embroidery stitches.

Preparing the Fabrics

We recommend that you use 100% cotton fabrics. Cottons are easy to work with, a cinch to care for, and available in an amazing variety of colors and prints.

Since these quilts are being made for babies, there is a very good chance that they will, at some point, need to be laundered—perhaps many times! For this reason, we recommend that you prewash the fabrics you plan to use in your quilt.

Sewing and Pressing

You'll be sewing the pieces, units, rows, blocks, and borders of these quilts together using a ¼" seam allowance. Your sewing machine may have a ¼"-wide foot attachment to help achieve an accurate ¼" seam. Press each seam as it's sewn. Press carefully, with an up-and-down, rather than a side-to-side, motion, which will pull the pieces out of shape and distort those nice, straight seams.

To help you, we've included pressing arrows in the project illustrations, indicating the best direction to press the seam allowances. Sometimes you'll press the seam allowances open to reduce the bulk when lots of seams come together.

Sew-and-Flip Technique

You'll *love* this easy, efficient method for piecing half-square triangles to the corners of squares and rectangles.

1. Cut the numbers and sizes of squares and rectangles (if needed) listed in the project cutting instructions. Draw a diagonal line from corner to corner on the wrong side of each small square.

2. Place a marked square, right sides together, with the appropriate rectangle or larger square, aligning the corners and edges as directed in the project instructions.

3. Sew directly on the marked line. (We like to place a pin on either side of the line so the small square doesn't shift.) Trim the excess corner fabric with your scissors or rotary cutter, leaving a ¼" seam allowance. Press the seam allowances toward the new, small triangle. Repeat to sew, trim, and press additional squares to the unit as instructed.

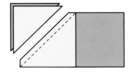

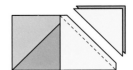

Adding Appliqués

When the projects included appliqués, we fused them to our quilts using lightweight fusible web, and finished the edges with a machine blanket stitch—or occasionally a small, tight zigzag or satin stitch—in thread that matched or contrasted with the appliqué fabric, depending upon the effect we wished to achieve. If you prefer, you can use fusible web, and then finish the edges of the appliqués by hand using a blanket stitch worked in cotton embroidery thread such as pearl cotton. The pattern pieces are already reversed for these fusible methods.

Needle Down Works Best

When using a decorative machine stitch, such as the blanket stitch, zigzag stitch, or satin stitch to finish the edges of your appliqués, use the needle-down function on your sewing machine, if your machine has this option. Turning corners and pivoting will be so much easier!

If you enjoy traditional hand appliqué, you'll need to reverse all pattern pieces and add a 3/16" to 1/4" seam allowance when you cut out the fabric shapes. The fabric amounts for appliqués in the materials lists have a bit of leeway to allow for this.

Curves Ahead!

Keep a small pair of sharp, curve-bladed manicuring scissors in your sewing room for cutting templates with curvy edges.

Placing the Appliqués

The step-by-step instructions for each quilt with appliqué include a placement diagram to help you position the appliqués. This diagram will help you with positioning and indicate the order in which to place the pieces by numbering them in a logical sequence. This is important, as shapes often overlap; the numbering system helps you to plan ahead for these overlaps. Dashed lines on the pattern pieces indicate where overlaps occur.

Once you're satisfied with the placement, begin bonding the pieces permanently in place. We like to place the unappliquéd block, border, or corner square on the ironing board. Once we've positioned the appliqués, the iron is close at hand: no lost or displaced pieces.

If you haven't already, remove the protective paper from the fusible web on the back of the fabric, reposition the appliqué, and apply pressure with a hot iron. Be sure to follow the manufacturer's instructions in terms of temperature and duration.

Peeling the Paper . . . with a Pin!

Allow the fabric to cool completely before attempting to remove the protective paper from the fusible web. If you're having difficulty, scratch the paper in a straight line with a pin—works like a charm, especially on small pieces.

Machine Stitching

Chris, who did all the machine appliqué on the quilts, did so *before* the blocks were assembled, to reduce the amount of fabric she would need to handle at the sewing machine. In preparation, she backed each block or border with tear-away stabilizer to keep the fabric from puckering (see "Resources" on page 11). We've included yardages for stabilizer in the materials list for each quilt that includes appliqué.

Choose all the threads—color and type—before you begin stitching. Cotton (50 weight) is perfect; not only is it strong and easy to work with, but it comes in a rainbow of colors, both solid and variegated. If you prefer that the stitching be subtler, select a thread close in color to the appliqué fabric. If you intend the stitching to be more of a design element, choose a contrasting thread.

Equip your machine with a topstitch or embroidery needle for doing the blanket or other decorative machine stitching around the appliqué shapes. These needles have larger eyes and a deeper groove, which help the thread pass through several layers without shredding.

Practice a bit using scraps from fabrics that have been prepped for fusing. Experiment with the length and width of the stitch until you find a look you like.

Finishing

The following techniques will help you transform that lovely quilt top into a beautifully textured, neatly finished, and attractively labeled future heirloom.

Layering and Basting

It's typical to cut the batting and backing somewhat larger than the quilt top to allow for any take up that might occur when the piece is quilted. For these small quilts, we've allowed an extra 4".

We basted the smaller quilts right on the design wall using basting spray. Place the backing (wrong side up) on the wall, spray with basting spray, then add the batting. Spray with basting spray again, then add the quilt top (right side up). If you prefer, you can use traditional thread or pin basting for the larger quilts.

If the instructions for your quilt call for a pieced backing, find and mark the midpoint along the lengthwise grain (selvage edge). Divide the fabric across the width (from selvage to selvage) at this point. Remove the selvages from both pieces, and sew them together side by side using a ½" seam allowance. Press the seam allowances open. If instructed, turn the backing so the seam runs horizontally for basting.

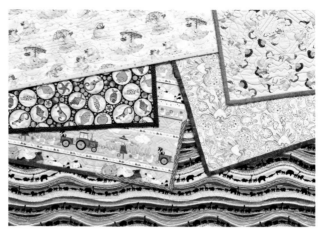

Theme and novelty prints make great choices for the backing, and add extra visual stimulation for the tiny recipient.

Quilting

We've included suggestions for quilting with each project, along with a nice, juicy detail photo of Chris's lovely machine work. Here are some additional, general thoughts on quilting.

- The sky's the limit when it comes to selecting quilting threads: cottons, rayons, metallics, solids, variegated colors . . . don't be afraid to try something new.

- When working with monofilament, increase your stitch length slightly. Sometimes monofilament has a tendency to stretch and may cause puckering; a larger stitch helps prevent this.

- If you plan to mark your quilting design on the quilt top, test your marking tool(s) on scraps of the fabrics you've used in the quilt. You want to be sure the marks will wash out easily.

- When placing border-quilting designs, work out the corner turns and the midpoints of each border first, and then fill in the rest, adjusting as necessary. Chris drew out many of her border designs on special tear-away tracing paper, which she removed after the quilting was done (see "Resources" on page 11).

Incorporating a Label and Sleeve

Although we hope that these quilts will be used and loved, we realize that some new parents like to display them, at least for a little while. That means adding a sleeve for hanging. Once the sleeve is made, we like to attach it to the quilt while adding the binding: saves a step! By incorporating the label into the sleeve, yet another step is eliminated.

A label is a must for any quilt, but never so much as when the quilt is made to celebrate such a landmark occasion. We recommend that any basic label include the name of the quilt, your name, the name of the quilter (if someone else does the honors), and the date the quilt was finished. Nowadays, it's a good idea to include an email address or other return address, just in case the quilt goes astray. For a baby quilt, you'll also want to record the name of the child, the date and place of birth, the parents' names, and any other pertinent details.

1. For a sleeve that finishes approximately 4" wide, cut a piece of fabric 9" x the width of the quilt. The backing fabric makes a good choice, but you can use leftovers from the front of the quilt or any other fabric from your stash, piecing it if necessary.

2. Turn the short raw edges of the sleeve fabric under ¼", and then ¼" again; press. Topstitch or zigzag the hems on both ends with thread to match the sleeve fabric.

3. Compose your label on the computer, adding all the necessary information. Frame it if you like, and add a little image that reflects the theme of the quilt. The text on the label should not be longer than 4" in order to be visible when the sleeve is folded and sewn to the quilt. The Internet offers lots of copyright-free art that you can use for this purpose; enlarge or reduce it as needed.

4. Select a treated-fabric product that can be used in your printer (see "Resources," opposite). Follow the manufacturer's instructions to transfer the printed label to the fabric.

5. Center the label right side up on the right side of the sleeve, dropping the label approximately ¼" from the top raw edge of the sleeve fabric;

pin. Stitch the sides and the bottom edge of the label to the sleeve with a zigzag stitch.

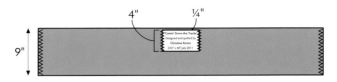

6. Fold the sleeve in half lengthwise, wrong sides together, and press.

Label on "Comin' Down the Tracks"

Adding the Binding

The quilts in this book are finished with double-fold binding, in most cases cut from the crosswise grain (across the width) of the binding fabric.

1. Trim the excess batting and backing on all sides so that it extends approximately ⅛" beyond the raw edge of the quilt top.

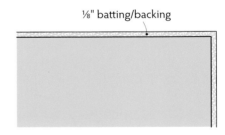

2. If adding a hanging sleeve, turn the quilt sandwich over and center the sleeve along the top edge, aligning the raw edges of the sleeve with the trimmed raw edges of the backing; machine baste to secure.

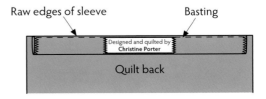

3. Working from the front of the quilt, place the raw edges of the binding even with the raw edge of the quilt top. Proceed with stitching the binding. If you need directions for making and attaching the binding, you can download free information at ShopMartingale.com/HowToQuilt. For an easy way to finish your binding, see Chris's tip, below.

For a No-Pin Finish . . .

Try Chris's no-pin technique for finishing off your binding. After sewing the binding to the quilt by machine, use a medium-hot iron to press the binding outward, away from the quilt center. Turn the quilt over and adhere ¼"-wide fusible tape within the seam allowance on the back of the quilt (see "Resources" at right). Remove the protective paper from the tape, fold the binding to the back of the quilt, and press, mitering the corners as you go. Finish by hand sewing the binding to the back of the quilt as usual.

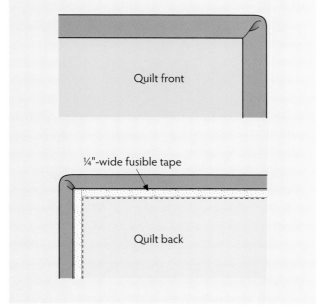

Quilt front

¼"-wide fusible tape

Quilt back

RESOURCES

Blumenthal Lansing
Crafter's Images PhotoFabric
www.blumenthallansing.com

The Cotton Patch
Cotty threads and fabric
www.cottonpatch.co.uk

Creative Grids
rulers
www.international@checkerdist.com
www.creativegrids.com

Golden Threads
quilting paper
www.goldenthreads.com

Husqvarna Viking
sewing machines
www.husqvarnaviking.com

Pellon
Stitch-N-Tear stabilizer
Wonder-Under fusible web
www.pellonideas.com

Superior Threads
Thread for machine quilting
www.superiorthreads.com

The Warm Company
Lite Steam-A-Seam 2
¼"-wide fusible tape
www.warmcompany.com

Designed and made by Darra Williamson; machine appliquéd and quilted by Christine Porter

rubber duckies

Quilt size: 34¾" x 43¼"
Finished block size: 6" x 6"
Number of blocks: 18

▼▼▼

Whimsical baby ducks bob across the surface of this adorable quilt, while its bright color scheme makes it ideal for a little one of either gender. A ⅜"-wide folded insert keeps the duckies corralled and adds a delightful touch of dimension.

Materials

Yardages are based on fabrics that measure 42" wide.

1⅛ yards *total* of assorted blue, blue-green, and yellow-green prints for background (sky and water)
1⅛ yards of aqua print for setting triangles and outer border
⅝ yard *total* of assorted yellow-print scraps for body and wing appliqués
¼ yard of multicolored small-scale plaid for folded inset border
⅛ yard *total* of assorted orange-print scraps for bill appliqués
4" x 4" scrap of black fabric for eye appliqués
½ yard of yellow dotted print for binding
1⅜ yards of fabric for backing
39" x 48" piece of batting
1⅛ yards of 18"-wide lightweight fusible web
1⅛ yards of 13"-wide tear-away stabilizer
Threads in assorted yellows and oranges for blanket-stitch appliqué

Cutting

Measurements include ¼"-wide seam allowances. Cut all strips on the crosswise grain (from selvage to selvage). Use the appliqué patterns on page 17.

From the assorted blue, blue-green, and yellow-green prints for background, cut a *total* of:

18 squares, 6½" x 6½", for sky
18 squares, 4½" x 4½", for water

From the assorted orange-print scraps, cut a *total* of:
17 bill appliqués and 1 reverse bill appliqué

From the assorted yellow-print scraps, cut a *total* of:
17 body appliqués and 1 reverse body appliqué
17 wing appliqués and 1 reverse wing appliqué

From the black scrap, cut:
18 eye appliqués

From the multicolored small-scale plaid, cut:
4 strips, 1¼" x 42"

From the aqua print, cut:
1 strip, 11" x 42"; crosscut into 3 squares, 11" x 11". Cut each square into quarters diagonally to make a total of 12 quarter-square triangles. (You'll have 2 triangles left over.)*
2 squares, 7" x 7"; cut each square in half diagonally to make a total of 4 half-square triangles.*
4 strips, 4½" x 42"

From the yellow dotted print, cut:
5 strips, 2½" x 42"

*These triangles are cut oversized; you'll trim them after completing the quilt top.

Go with the Fabric

You may prefer to disregard the grain line when cutting some of the sky and water squares to take advantage of a directional print. Simply place your ruler on the fabric to get the desired effect, and fussy cut the square as shown. When you've assembled the background, before adding the appliqués, baste around the perimeter of the block a scant ¼" from the raw edges. This will help stabilize the bias edges until you're ready to sew the block into the quilt.

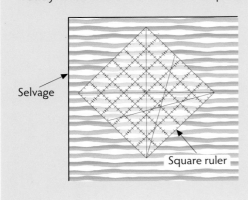

Selvage

Square ruler

Making the Blocks

1. Turn a 6½" sky square on point. Referring to the "Sew-and-Flip Technique" on page 7, sew a 4½" water square to the bottom corner of the larger square; trim and press. Be sure to pay attention to the direction of the print if you've fussy cut either of the squares as described in "Go with the Fabric," above.

2. Fold the background block into quarters diagonally; finger-press lightly. This marks the center of the block to assist you with appliqué placement.

Flip It!

Sometimes the "right" side is the "wrong" side! If the fabric you're considering doesn't provide the proper degree of contrast, flip it over and consider the reverse side. Often, the value (or the blurred motif) on the back of a print is *just* different enough to make it the perfect choice.

3. Referring to the appliqué placement diagram below, position a duck bill, body, wing, and eye appliqué on the pieced background block in the order shown.

4. Following the manufacturer's instructions for the fusible web, adhere the appliqués to the block.

5. Secure the appliqués to the block using a machine or hand blanket stitch. Rather than blanket stitching the eye, try a small spiral or X in the center.

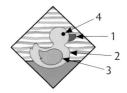

Appliqué placement

6. Repeat steps 1–5 to make a total of 17 regular blocks and 1 reverse block.

rubber duckies

Assembling the Quilt

Do not trim the oversized setting triangles until instructed to do so in step 3.

1. Arrange the appliquéd blocks, the quarter-square (side) setting triangles, and the half-square (corner) setting triangles in diagonal rows as shown in the quilt assembly diagram.

2. Sew the blocks and the side setting triangles together into diagonal rows; press as shown. Sew the rows together; press. Add the corner triangles; press.

Quilt assembly

3. Carefully straighten the edges of the quilt top by trimming ⅝" from the outer corners of the blocks. The trim is bigger than the standard ¼". This ensures that when the folded insert is sewn, it does not cover the points of the blocks. Square the quilt corners.

Adding the Folded Insert and Border

1. Measure the quilt through the center from top to bottom. Trim two 1¼"-wide plaid strips to this measurement for the side inserts. Measure the quilt through the center from side to side. Trim the remaining two 1¼"-wide plaid strips to this measurement for the top and bottom inserts.

2. With wrong sides together, fold each 1¼"-wide plaid strip in half lengthwise; press.

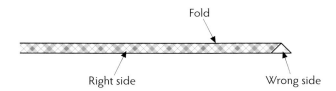

Fold

Right side   Wrong side

3. With raw edges aligned, use a basting stitch and scant ¼" seam allowance to stitch the side folded-insert strips to the sides of the quilt.

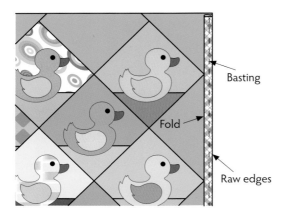

Repeat to sew the top and bottom folded inserts to the top and bottom of the quilt.

4. Measure the quilt through the center from top to bottom. Trim two 4½"-wide aqua strips to this measurement. Referring to the quilt plan, and with right sides together, sew the trimmed strips to the sides of the quilt. Press the seam allowances toward the border, making sure that the folded inserts remain facing the center of the quilt.

5. Measure the quilt through the center from side to side, including the borders you've just added. Trim the remaining two 4½"-wide aqua strips to this measurement, and then sew the strips to the top and bottom of the quilt, again making sure the folded inserts remain facing the center of the quilt; press.

Finishing the Quilt

Refer to "Finishing" (page 9) as needed. For step-by-step instructions on quilt-finishing techniques (layering, basting, quilting, binding, and much more), please visit ShopMartingale.com/HowtoQuilt.

1. Layer the backing, batting, and quilt top; baste.

2. Hand or machine quilt as desired.

3. Use the 2½"-wide yellow dotted strips to finish the edges of your quilt, incorporating a label and sleeve.

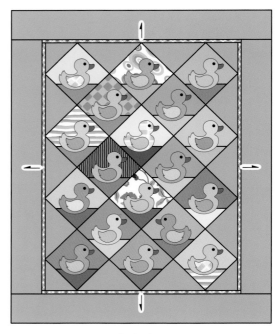

Quilt plan

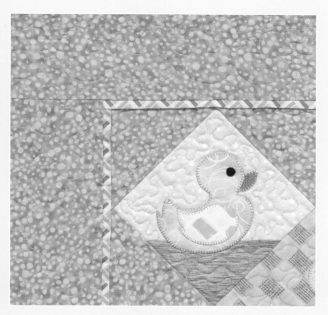

Detail of quilting on "Rubber Duckies"

SUGGESTIONS FOR QUILTING

Chris began by using clear monofilament to quilt in the ditch along all the diagonal seams. Once the quilt was anchored, she used matching thread to stitch right around the edges of the duck, bill, and wing appliqués, and black thread to stitch around the eyes.

Switching to blue thread, Chris free-motion quilted wavy blue lines under each duck to represent water, and added various swirly designs suggested by the sky fabric to represent clouds, wind, rain, and so on. The setting triangles were free-motion quilted in wavy lines using matching blue-green thread.

Clear monofilament was used to quilt in the ditch of the outer-border seam. For a final, whimsical touch, ducks—free-motion quilted in yellow thread—parade nose to nose around the outer border, with squiggly lines filling the background.

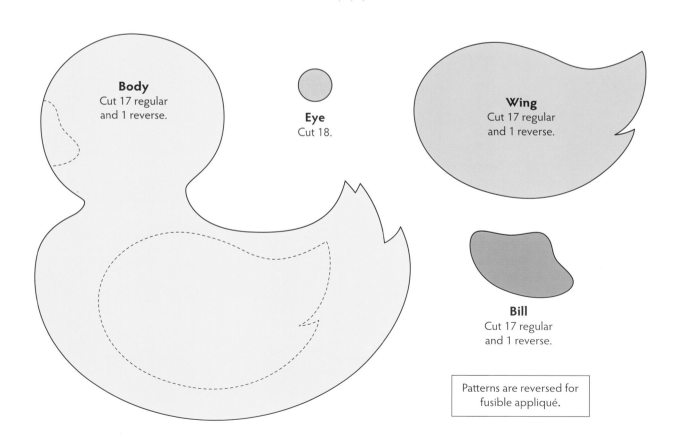

Body
Cut 17 regular
and 1 reverse.

Eye
Cut 18.

Wing
Cut 17 regular
and 1 reverse.

Bill
Cut 17 regular
and 1 reverse.

Patterns are reversed for
fusible appliqué.

Designed, made, and machine quilted by Christine Porter

fresh as a daisy

Quilt size: 32⅜" x 38¾"
Finished block size: 4½" x 4½"
Number of blocks: 30
∗Charm-square friendly ∗

▼▼▼

A color scheme reminiscent of daisies on a summer morning suggested the name of this cheerful little quilt, and a charming daisy quilting motif reinforces the theme. It's the *perfect* choice for a new quilter, and its easy and efficient strip-pieced construction all but guarantees an "on-time" delivery!

Materials

Yardages are based on fabrics that measure 42" wide.

1 yard of blue tone-on-tone print for setting triangles and binding

⅝ yard *total* of assorted blue prints for blocks

½ yard *total* of assorted yellow prints for blocks

⅜ yard *each* of 2 assorted blue-and-white prints for blocks*

1⅓ yards of fabric for backing

37" x 43" piece of batting

*If you prefer a scrappier look, you can use more than two blue-and-white fabrics. You can even substitute twenty 5" charm squares for this yardage.

Cutting

Measurements include ¼" seam allowance. Cut all strips on the crosswise grain (from selvage to selvage).

From the assorted yellow prints, cut a *total* of:
7 strips, 2" x 42"

From the assorted blue prints, cut a *total* of:
8 strips, 2" x 42"

From *each* blue-and-white print, cut:
2 strips, 5" x 42"; crosscut into 10 squares, 5" x 5" (20 total)

From the blue tone-on-tone print, cut:
2 strips, 9" x 42"; crosscut into 5 squares, 9" x 9". Cut each square into quarters diagonally to make a total of 20 quarter-square triangles. (You'll have 2 triangles left over.)*

2 squares, 5½" x 5½"; cut each square in half diagonally to make a total of 4 half-square triangles.*

4 strips, 2½" x 42"

*These triangles are cut oversized; you'll trim them after completing the quilt top.

Making the Blocks

1. With right sides together, sew a 2"-wide yellow strip between two 2"-wide assorted blue strips; press. Make three scrappy strip sets. Cut the strip sets into a total of 60 segments, 2" wide.

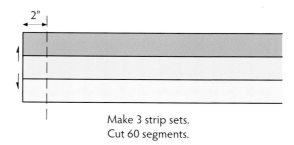

Make 3 strip sets.
Cut 60 segments.

2. With right sides together, sew a 2"-wide blue strip between two 2"-wide assorted yellow strips; press. Make two scrappy strip sets. Cut the strip sets into a total of 30 segments, 2" wide.

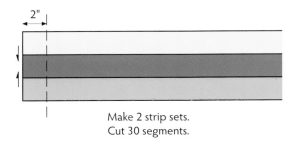

Make 2 strip sets.
Cut 30 segments.

3. Sew a segment from step 2 between two segments from step 1; press. Repeat to make 30 scrappy blocks.

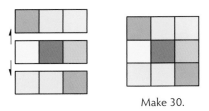

Make 30.

Assembling the Quilt

Do not trim the oversized setting triangles until instructed to do so in step 3.

1. Arrange the blocks, the 5" blue-and-white squares, the quarter-square (side) setting triangles, and the half-square (corner) setting triangles in diagonal rows as shown in the quilt assembly diagram above right, alternating the placement of the two different 5" squares.

2. Sew the blocks, the squares, and the side setting triangles together into diagonal rows; press. Sew the rows together; press. Add the corner triangles; press.

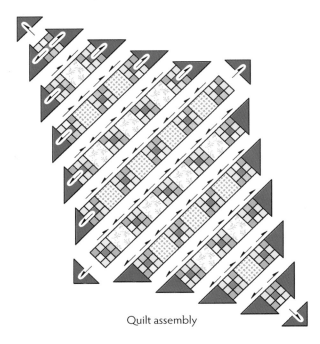

Quilt assembly

3. Carefully straighten the edges of the quilt top by trimming a generous ¼" from the outer corners of the blocks. Square the quilt corners.

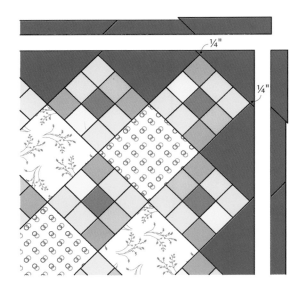

fresh as a daisy

Detail of quilting on "Fresh as a Daisy"

SUGGESTIONS FOR QUILTING

Rather than stitching in the ditch with clear monofilament to anchor the seams, Chris used a color-coordinated variegated thread to quilt wavy lines right along the outside edges of the blocks in both directions. This not only stabilized the quilt, but added a decorative touch to offset the straight lines of the pieced quilt top. (Some machines have a programmed stitch that you can use for this; set the stitch length at 3.) She then used the same thread and wavy-line motif to stitch an X through each block, passing through the center of each small blue square.

The setting squares were free-motion quilted in a double-daisy motif using white thread; half of the same motif was stitched in matching blue thread to fill the setting triangles.

Finishing the Quilt

Refer to "Finishing" (page 9) as needed. For step-by-step instructions on quilt-finishing techniques (layering, basting, quilting, binding, and much more), please visit ShopMartingale.com/HowtoQuilt.

1. Layer the backing, batting, and quilt top; baste.

2. Hand or machine quilt as desired.

3. Use the 2½"-wide blue tone-on-tone strips to finish the edges of your quilt, incorporating a label and sleeve.

Quilt plan

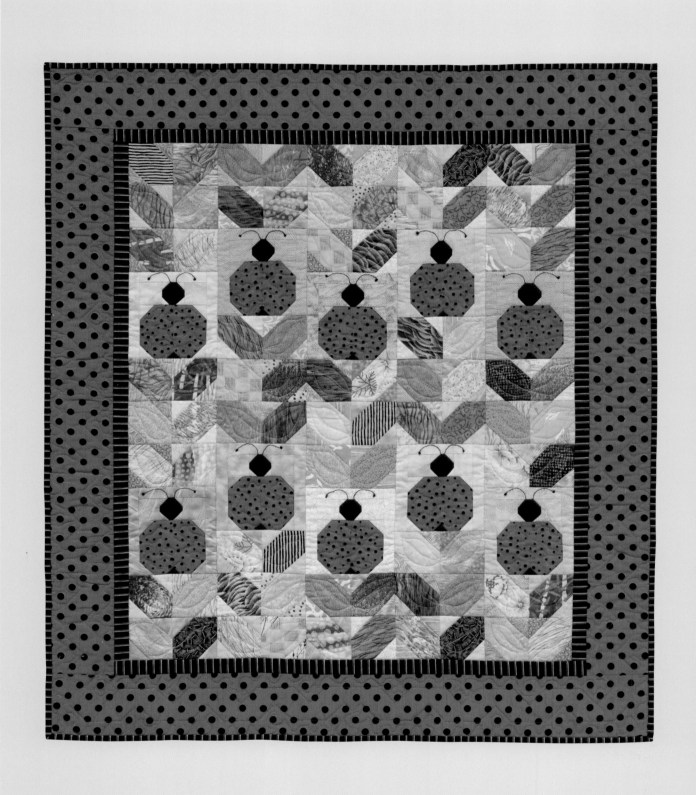

Designed and made by Darra Williamson; machine quilted by Christine Porter

ladybug! ladybug!

Quilt size: 41" x 47"
Finished block size:
Ladybug: 6" x 6" | Leaf: 3" x 3"
Total number of blocks:
Ladybug: 10 | Leaf: 80
Charm-square friendly

Ladybugs (called *ladybirds* in Britain) are recognized in many cultures as harbingers of luck and of love—fine things to wish for any new babe. With its super-simple piecing and staggered-for-ease set, this clever quilt goes together with surprising efficiency. A bright, cheery palette and touches of whimsical embroidery make it perfect for introducing *your* special little one to the classic childhood rhyme.

Materials

Yardages are based on fabrics that measure 42" wide.

1⅓ yards of red large-scale polka-dot print for outer border
1 yard *total* of assorted light- and medium-blue prints for Ladybug and Leaf blocks
1 yard *total* of assorted medium- and dark-green prints for Leaf blocks*
⅓ yard of red small-scale polka-dot print for Ladybug blocks
⅛ yard of black solid for Ladybug blocks
⅝ yard of black striped fabric for inner border and binding
2⅞ yards of fabric for backing (horizontal seam)
44" x 51" piece of batting
Black embroidery floss

You can substitute 80 charm squares, 5" x 5", and trim to 3½" square for this yardage.

Cutting

Measurements include ¼" seam allowance. Cut all strips on the crosswise grain (from selvage to selvage) unless otherwise noted.

From the assorted light- and medium-blue prints, cut:
80 pairs of matching 2" x 2" squares (160 total)
Then cut the following matching pieces for *each* of the 10 Ladybug blocks:

4 squares, 1½" x 1½"
4 squares, 1" x 1"
2 squares, 2" x 2"
1 rectangle, 1¼" x 5"
2 rectangles, 1¼" x 6½"

From the red small-scale polka-dot print, cut:
3 strips, 2¾" x 42"; crosscut into 20 rectangles, 2¾" x 4¼"

From the black solid, cut:
1 strip, 1" x 42"; crosscut into 20 squares, 1" x 1"
1 strip, 2" x 42"; crosscut into 10 squares, 2" x 2"

From the assorted medium- and dark-green prints, cut a *total* of:
80 squares, 3½" x 3½"

From the black striped fabric, cut:
4 strips, 1½" x 42"
5 strips, 2½" x 42"

From the *lengthwise grain* of the red large-scale polka-dot print, cut:
4 strips, 4¾" x the fabric length

Making the Ladybug Blocks

1. Referring to "Sew-and-Flip Technique" (page 7), sew matching 1½" blue squares to the left top and bottom corners of two 2¾" x 4¼" red small-scale polka-dot rectangles; trim and press.

 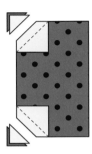

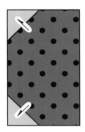

Make 2.

2. Rotate one unit from step 1 as shown. Using the sew-and-flip technique, sew a 1" black square to the remaining lower corner; trim and press. Make one each.

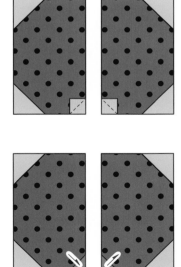

3. Sew the units from step 2 together as shown. Press the center seam allowances open.

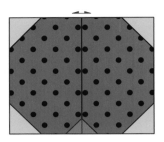

4. Using the sew-and-flip technique, sew 1" matching blue squares to opposite corners of a 2" black square; trim and press. Repeat to sew 1" matching blue squares to the remaining corners; press. (See "When *Not* to Trim" on page 55 for advice about trimming these small squares.)

5. Sew the unit from step 4 between two matching 2" blue squares; press. Sew a matching 1¼" x 5" blue strip to the top edge of the unit; press.

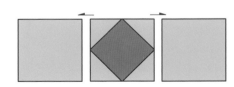

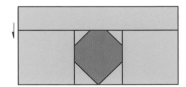

6. Sew the units from step 3 and step 5 together as shown; press.

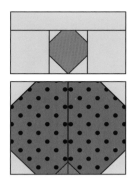 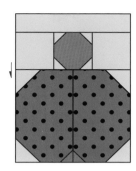

7. Sew the unit from step 6 between two matching 1¼" x 6½" blue strips; press.

8. Repeat steps 1–7 to make a total of 10 Ladybug blocks.

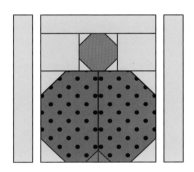

Make 10.

Making the Leaf Blocks

Using the sew-and-flip technique, sew matching 2" blue squares to opposite corners of a 3½" green square; trim and press. Make 80.

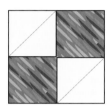 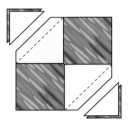

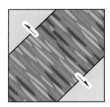

Make 80.

Assembling the Quilt

1. Arrange two Ladybug blocks and 16 Leaf blocks *each* in five vertical rows as shown in the quilt assembly diagram on page 26. When you're satisfied with the arrangement, sew the Leaf blocks together in pairs, referring to "Re-press for Success" on page 26. Press the seam allowances open.

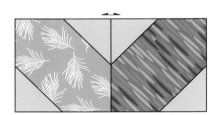

 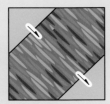

Re-press for Success

Before sewing the pair of Leaf blocks together, re-press the top diagonal seam allowances toward the leaf fabric on one block. When you pin the two blocks together, the two diagonal seams will nest, making for a nice, neat match.

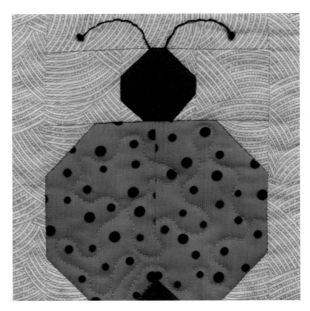

Detail of embroidery on "Ladybug! Ladybug!"

2. Sew leaf units and Ladybug blocks together into vertical rows as shown; press. Sew the rows together; press.

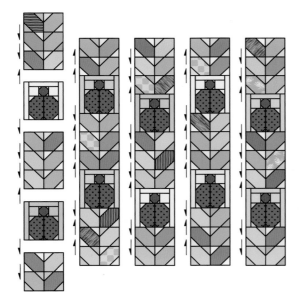

Quilt assembly

3. Referring to the photo (page 22), use one strand of black embroidery floss and a stem stitch to embroider the antennae on each Ladybug block as shown. Use two strands of black embroidery floss to make a French knot at the end of each antenna.

Adding the Borders

1. Measure the quilt through the center from top to bottom. Trim two 1½"-wide black striped strips to this measurement. With right sides together, sew the strips to the sides of the quilt. Press the seam allowances toward the border.

2. Measure the quilt through the center from side to side, including the borders you've just added. Trim the remaining 1½"-wide black striped strips to this measurement, and sew them to the top and bottom of the quilt; press.

3. Measure the quilt through the center from top to bottom. Trim two 4¾"-wide red large-scale polka-dot strips to this measurement. Referring to the quilt plan and with right sides together, sew these strips to the sides of the quilt. Press the seam allowances toward the border.

4. Measure the quilt through the center from side to side, including the borders you've just added. Trim the remaining two 4¾"-wide red large-scale polka-dot strips to this measurement, and sew them to the top and bottom of the quilt; press.

Detail of quilting on "Ladybug! Ladybug!"

SUGGESTIONS FOR QUILTING

Chris used clear monofilament to stitch in the ditch along the seams between the vertical and then the horizontal rows to anchor the quilt center. She continued by stitching in the ditch around the ladybug shapes (including the heads) and the individual leaves.

Switching to green thread, Chris free-motion quilted a simple leaf design in each Leaf block. She used red thread to stipple a design around each ladybug's black spots, and pale-blue thread to stipple the ladybug backgrounds.

After using the clear monofilament to quilt in the ditch on both sides of the inner border, Chris added the finishing touches by adapting a leaf motif from the blocks and free-motion quilting it in the outer border with bright-red thread.

Finishing the Quilt

Refer to "Finishing" (page 9) as needed. For step-by-step instructions on quilt-finishing techniques (layering, basting, quilting, binding, and much more), please visit ShopMartingale.com/HowtoQuilt.

1. Lay out the backing so the seam runs horizontally and add the batting and quilt top; baste.

2. Hand or machine quilt as desired.

3. Use the 2½"-wide black striped strips to finish the edges of your quilt, incorporating a label and sleeve.

Quilt plan

Designed, made, and machine quilted by Christine Porter

goodnight, sweetheart

Quilt size: 40½" x 52½"
Finished block size: 6" x 6"
Number of blocks:
Heart: 18 | Chain: 17

Here's another great choice for the beginning quilter . . . and for easing a precious little one gently to sleep. The pieced Heart blocks go together like a dream with the quick-and-easy sew-and-flip technique; strip piecing makes the Chain blocks a breeze as well. Chris has used a delicate-pink color scheme for her version of this adorable quilt, but you can substitute blue or any other color you choose to make this quilt a perfect fit for any nursery.

Materials

Yardages are based on fabrics that measure 42" wide.

1⅜ yards of white-with-pink floral for large Heart and alternate blocks

⅞ yard of light-pink tone-on-tone print for outer border and small Heart blocks

⅔ yard of medium-pink tone-on-tone print for inner border and binding

⅓ yard *each* of 6 assorted deep-pink prints for large and small Heart blocks

¼ yard of light-pink print for Chain blocks

¼ yard of medium-pink print for Chain blocks

¼ yard of medium-dark pink-swirl print for Chain blocks

2⅝ yards of fabric for backing (horizontal seam)

45" x 57" piece of batting

Cutting

Measurements include ¼" seam allowances. Cut all strips on the crosswise grain (from selvage to selvage).

From *each* of the 6 assorted deep-pink prints, cut:
1 strip, 6½" x 42"; crosscut into 3 rectangles, 5½" x 6½" (18 total)
1 strip, 1½" x 42"; crosscut into 6 rectangles, 1½" x 3½" (36 total)

From *each* of 4 of the assorted deep-pink prints, cut:
1 rectangle, 3¾" x 4½" (4 total)
2 rectangles, 1¼" x 2½" (8 total)

From the white-with-pink floral, cut:
9 strips, 1½" x 42"; crosscut *3* strips into 72 squares, 1½" x 1½"
4 strips, 3½" x 42"; crosscut into 36 squares, 3½" x 3½"
7 strips, 2½" x 42"; crosscut *3* strips into 34 squares, 2½" x 2½"

From the light-pink print, cut:
3 strips, 1½" x 42"

From the medium-pink print, cut:
3 strips, 1½" x 42"

From the medium-dark pink-swirl print, cut:
2 strips, 2½" x 42"

From the medium-pink tone-on-tone print, cut:
4 strips, 1½" x 42"
6 strips, 2½" x 42"

From the light-pink tone-on-tone print, cut:
1 strip, 1¼" x 42"; crosscut into 16 squares, 1¼" x 1¼"
1 strip, 2½" x 42"; crosscut into 8 squares, 2½" x 2½"
5 strips, 4½" x 42"

Making the Large Heart Blocks

For each block, you'll need one 5½" x 6½" rectangle and two 1½" x 3½" rectangles cut from the same deep-pink print.

1. Referring to "Sew-and-Flip Technique" (page 7), sew 3½" white-with-pink squares to the bottom corners of a 5½" x 6½" deep-pink rectangle; trim and press.

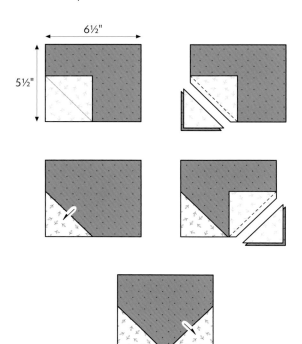

2. Using the sew-and-flip technique, sew 1½" white-with-pink squares to opposite ends of a 1½" x 3½" deep-pink rectangle, matching the rectangle from step 1; trim and press. Make two matching units.

Make 2.

3. Sew the two units from step 2 together side by side; press.

4. Sew the unit from step 3 to the top edge of the matching unit from step 1; press.

5. Repeat steps 1–4 to make a total of 18 large Heart blocks.

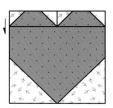

Make 18.

Making the Small Heart Blocks

For each block, you'll need one 3¾" x 4½" rectangle and two 1¼" x 2½" rectangles cut from the same deep-pink print. Refer to the illustrations in "Making the Large Heart Blocks," steps 1–4 for guidance.

1. Using the sew-and-flip technique, sew 2½" light-pink tone-on-tone squares to the bottom corners of a 3¾" x 4½" deep-pink rectangle; trim and press.

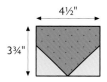

2. Sew 1¼" light-pink tone-on-tone squares to opposite ends of a 1¼" x 2½" deep-pink rectangle matching the rectangle from step 1; trim and press. Make two matching units.

3. Sew the two units from step 2 together side by side; press.

4. Sew the unit from step 3 to the top edge of the matching unit from step 1; press.

5. Repeat steps 1–4 to make a total of four small Heart blocks.

Make 4.

Making the Chain Blocks

1. With right sides together, sew a 1½"-wide light-pink strip and a 1½"-wide white-with-pink strip together along their long edges to make a strip set; press. Make three strip sets. Cut the strip sets into a total of 68 segments, 1½" wide.

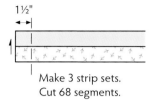

Make 3 strip sets.
Cut 68 segments.

2. Repeat step 1 using the 1½"-wide medium-pink strips and 1½"-wide white-with-pink strips. Make three strip sets; press. Cut the strip sets into a total of 68 segments, 1½" wide.

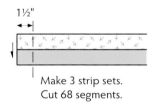

Make 3 strip sets.
Cut 68 segments.

3. Arrange one segment from step 1 and one segment from step 2 as shown. Sew the segments together; press. Make 68 units.

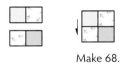

Make 68.

4. Sew a 2½" white-with-pink square between two units from step 3, rotating the units as shown; press. Make 34 rows.

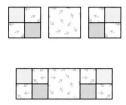

Make 34.

5. With right sides together, sew a 2½"-wide medium-dark pink-swirl strip between two 2½"-wide white-with-pink strips along their long edges to make a strip set; press. Make two strip sets. Cut the strip sets into a total of 17 segments, 2½" wide.

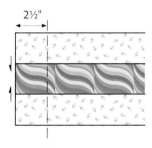

Make 2 strip sets.
Cut 17 segments.

6. Arrange one segment from step 5 between two rows from step 4, rotating the rows as shown. Sew the rows and segment together; press. Make a total of 17 Chain blocks.

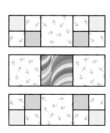
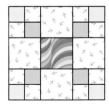

Make 17.

Assembling the Quilt

1. Arrange the large Heart blocks and the Chain blocks in seven horizontal rows of five blocks each, alternating the blocks as shown in the quilt assembly diagram.

2. Sew the blocks together into horizontal rows; press. Sew the rows together; press.

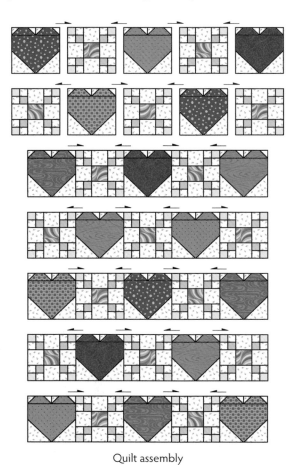

Quilt assembly

Adding the Borders

1. Sew the 1½"-wide medium-pink tone-on-tone strips together end to end using diagonal seams to make one long strip. Measure the quilt through the center from top to bottom, and cut two 1½"-wide medium-pink tone-on-tone strips to this measurement. With right sides together, sew the strips to the sides of the quilt. Press the seam allowances toward the border.

2. Measure the quilt through the center from side to side, including the borders you've just added. From the remaining 1½"-wide medium-pink tone-on-tone strip, cut two strips to this measurement and sew them to the top and bottom of the quilt; press.

3. Sew the 4½"-wide light-pink tone-on-tone strips together end to end using diagonal seams to make one long strip. Measure the quilt through the center from top to bottom, and cut two 4½"-wide light-pink tone-on-tone strips to this measurement. These will be the side borders.

4. Measure the quilt through the center from side to side. From the remaining 4½"-wide light-pink tone-on-tone strip, cut two strips to this measurement. These will be the top and bottom borders.

5. Sew the side border strips from step 3 to the sides of the quilt. Press the seam allowances toward the newly added border.

6. Sew a small Heart block to each end of each top and bottom border strip from step 6; press. Make two.

Make 2.

7. Referring to the quilt plan (opposite), sew the border units from step 6 to the top and bottom edges of the quilt; press.

Detail of quilting on "Goodnight, Sweetheart"

SUGGESTIONS FOR QUILTING

Chris used a color-coordinated variegated thread to quilt wavy lines in a large X through the pink squares in the Chain blocks. Switching to a light-pink thread, she repeated the process to quilt through the white-with-pink print squares, cutting across the corners of the Heart blocks to link the blocks together. The wavy lines soften the many straight lines and right angles of the pieced design.

Chris quilted the Heart blocks by stitching in the ditch around the heart shapes with clear monofilament, and then added two concentric heart motifs in the center of each Heart block with matching dark-pink thread.

The inner border was anchored in the ditch on both sides with clear monofilament, and the outer border was quilted in a complementary heart-and-diamond motif using medium-pink thread.

Finishing the Quilt

Refer to "Finishing" (page 9) as needed. For step-by-step instructions on quilt-finishing techniques (layering, basting, quilting, binding, and much more), please visit ShopMartingale.com/HowtoQuilt.

1. Lay out the backing so the seam runs horizontally and add the batting and quilt top; baste.

2. Hand or machine quilt as desired.

3. Use the 2½"-wide medium-pink tone-on-tone strips to finish the edges of your quilt, incorporating a label and sleeve.

Quilt plan

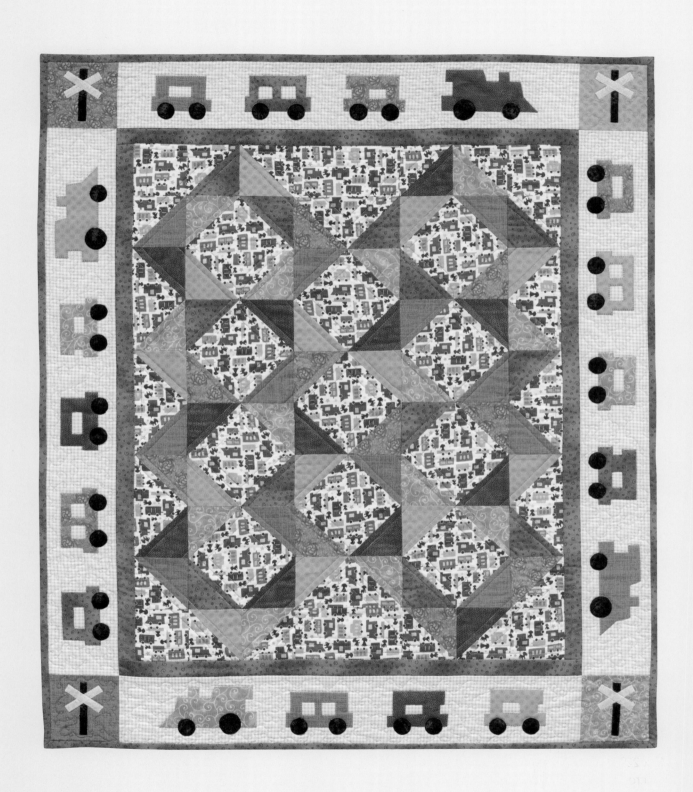

Designed, made, and machine quilted by Christine Porter

comin' down the tracks

Quilt size: 34½" x 40½"
Finished block size: 6" x 6"
Number of blocks: 11

▼▼▼

Choo choo! All aboard and away we go! What little one isn't fascinated by a train? Now you can make your own tiny conductor this brightly colored, railroad-themed quilt, complete with locomotives, carriage cars . . . even crossing signs to mark the corners. Chris staggered the super-easy Square-in-a-Square blocks to create the zigzag tracks, and added the appliqués with fusible web and simple decorative stitches. Couldn't be simpler!

Materials

Yardages are based on fabrics that measure 42" wide.

1 yard of multicolored train-themed print for blocks and background
⅝ yard of red tone-on-tone print for inner border and binding*
⅝ yard of green-and-white gingham for outer border
⅜ yard *each* of 2 assorted blue, red, and green tone-on-tone prints for blocks, corner squares, and locomotive and carriage appliqués (6 fabrics total)
¼ yard of black tone-on-tone print for wheel and crossing-sign appliqués
1" x 20" strip of white tone-on-tone print for crossing-sign appliqués
1⅜ yards of fabric for backing

39" x 45" piece of batting
1 yard of 18"-wide lightweight fusible web
1⅓ yards of 13"-wide tear-away stabilizer
Threads in assorted colors for blanket-stitch appliqué

*This can be one of the two red prints you use for the blocks.

Cutting

Measurements include ¼" seam allowance. Cut all strips on the crosswise grain (from selvage to selvage). Use the appliqué patterns on page 40.

From *each* of the 2 blue, red, and green tone-on-tone prints, cut:
1 strip, 3½" x 42"; crosscut into 10 squares, 3½" x 3½" (60 total)
1 square, 4" x 4" (6 total)

From the remaining blue, red, and green tone-on-tone prints, cut a *total* of:
1 square, 4½" x 4½", from each of 4 different fabrics (4 total)
3 locomotive appliqués and 1 reverse locomotive appliqué
5 carriage A appliqués
3 carriage B appliqués and 2 reverse carriage B appliqués
4 carriage C appliqués

From the multicolored train-themed print, cut:
2 strips, 6½" x 42"; crosscut into 11 squares, 6½" x 6½"
2 strips, 3½" x 42"; crosscut into:
    10 rectangles, 3½" x 6½"
    4 squares, 3½" x 3½"
1 strip, 4" x 42"; crosscut into 6 squares, 4" x 4"

Continued on page 36

From the black tone-on-tone print, cut:
4 large wheel appliqués
32 small wheel appliqués
1 strip, 1" x 15", for crossing-sign post appliqués

From the 1" x 20" white tone-on-tone print strip, cut:
8 rectangles, ⅜" x 2¼", for crossing-sign appliqués

From the red tone-on-tone print, cut:
4 strips, 1½" x 42"
5 strips, 2½" x 42"

From the green-and-white gingham, cut:
4 strips, 4½" x 42"

Making the Blocks

To duplicate the effect in the quilt photo (page 34), use at least one 3½" square of each color (red, green, and blue) in each block.

Referring to the "Sew-and-Flip Technique" on page 7, sew 3½" blue, red, or green squares to opposite corners of a 6½" train-print square; trim and press. Repeat to sew different 3½" squares to the remaining corners; trim and press. Make 11.

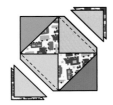

Make 11.

Making the Setting Units

1. Using the sew-and-flip technique, sew a 3½" blue, green, or red square to one end of a 3½" x 6½" train-print rectangle; trim and press. Sew a different 3½" blue, green, or red square to the other end of the rectangle; trim and press. Make eight flying-geese units.

Make 8.

2. Draw a diagonal line from corner to corner on the wrong side of a 4" train-print square. This will be your cutting line. Draw a line ¼" from the diagonal line on both sides as shown. These lines will be your sewing lines.

¼"

3. Place the marked square right sides together with a 4" blue, green, or red square. Sew directly on the two outermost lines. Cut the unit apart on the center diagonal line; press. You now have two identical half-square-triangle units. Trim each unit to measure 3½" x 3½".

4. Repeat steps 2 and 3 to make a total of 12 half-square-triangle units.

3½"

Make 12 units total.

Assembling the Quilt

1. Arrange the blocks, flying-geese units, half-square-triangle units, remaining 3½" x 6½" train-print rectangles, and the 3½" train-print squares as shown in the quilt assembly diagram.

2. When you're satisfied with the color placement, sew the pairs of half-square-triangle units at the top and bottom of rows 2 and 4 together as shown; press.

3. Sew the blocks, units, rectangles, and squares together to make five vertical rows; press.

4. Sew the vertical rows together; press.

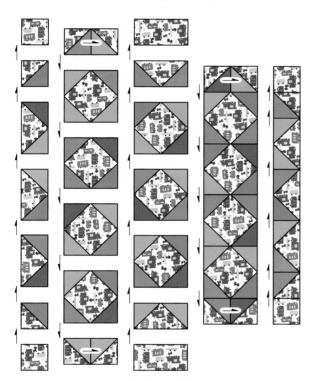

Quilt assembly

5. Measure the quilt through the center from top to bottom. Trim two 1½"-wide red tone-on-tone strips to this measurement and sew them to the sides of the quilt. Press the seam allowances toward the border.

6. Measure the quilt through the center from side to side, including the borders you've just added. Trim the remaining two 1½"-wide red tone-on-tone strips to this measurement, and sew them to the top and bottom of the quilt; press.

Appliquéing the Outer Border

Refer to "Adding Appliqués" (page 8) as needed for help with the following steps.

1. Measure the quilt through the center from top to bottom. Trim two 4½"-wide gingham strips to this measurement and label them side border strips.

2. Measure the quilt through the center from side to side. Trim the remaining two 4½"-wide gingham strips to this measurement, and label them top/bottom border strips.

3. Fold each gingham strip in half, and then in half again; finger-press lightly. This creates guide marks to assist you with appliqué placement. You'll use the longer strips for the side borders.

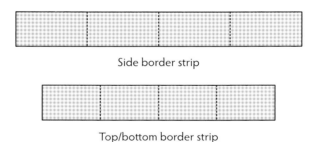

Side border strip

Top/bottom border strip

4. Referring to the side-border appliqué placement diagram, position one each of the locomotive, carriage B, and carriage C appliqués, and two carriage A appliqués on a side border strip as shown.

5. Following the manufacturer's instructions for the fusible web, adhere the appliqués to the border strip.

6. Secure the appliqués to the strip using a machine or hand blanket stitch.

7. Referring to the placement diagram, position the wheel appliqués: one small wheel at the front of the locomotive, one large wheel at the back, and eight small wheels on the carriages

as shown. Repeat steps 5 and 6 to fuse and stitch the appliqués in place, substituting a small zigzag stitch for the blanket stitch.

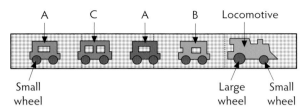

Side-border appliqué placement

8. Repeat steps 4–7 to appliqué a second side border.

9. Referring to the top-border appliqué placement diagram, position a locomotive and one each of carriages A–C on a top border strip as shown. Repeat steps 5 and 6 to fuse and stitch the appliqués to the border.

10. Referring to the placement diagram, position the wheel appliqués: one small wheel at the front of the locomotive, one large wheel at the back, and six small wheels on the carriages as shown. Repeat steps 5 and 6 to fuse and stitch the appliqués to the strip to complete the top border, substituting a small zigzag stitch for the blanket stitch.

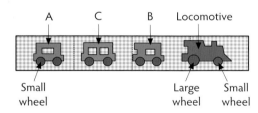

Top-border appliqué placement

11. Referring to the bottom-border appliqué placement diagram, fuse and stitch the reverse locomotive, a carriage C appliqué, the two reverse carriage B appliqués, and the remaining wheel appliqués to the bottom border strip.

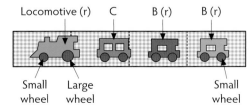

Bottom-border appliqué placement

Appliquéing the Corner Squares

Refer to "Adding Appliqués" as needed for help with the following steps.

1. From the 1" x 15" prepared black strip, cut four rectangles, ⅜" x 3".

2. Fold a 4½" blue, red, or green square in half vertically and horizontally; finger-press lightly. This marks the center of the block to assist you with appliqué placement.

3. Referring to the corner-square appliqué placement diagram below, position a ⅜" x 3" black rectangle and two ⅜" x 2¼" white rectangles on the folded corner square as shown.

4. Following the manufacturer's instructions for the fusible web, adhere the appliqués to the corner square.

5. Secure the appliqués to the square using a machine or hand blanket stitch.

6. Repeat steps 2–5 to make a total of four corner squares.

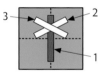

Corner-square appliqué placement

Adding the Outer Border

Refer to the quilt plan (opposite) for guidance in orienting the appliquéd border strips. The border strip with the appliqués reversed will be the bottom border.

1. Sew the appliquéd side border strips to the left and right edges of the quilt. Press the seam allowances toward the appliquéd borders.

2. Sew an appliquéd corner square to each short end of the top border strip; press. Sew the strip to the top of the quilt; press.

Detail of quilting on "Comin' Down the Tracks"

SUGGESTIONS FOR QUILTING

Quilting is easy peasy for this quilt: straight-line quilting in the blocks with puffy, stippled clouds in the border. Chris used colorful cotton thread that matched the colors of the quilt for all the visible stitching; variegated thread makes a fun choice, too.

Using the width of the quilting foot as a guide, Chris quilted ¼" from the inside edges of the zigzag triangles, setting triangles, and center squares of the Square-in-a-Square blocks. She added a second line of stitching ¼" inside the first lines in the setting triangles and blocks. Next, she quilted in the ditch using clear monofilament to stabilize the inner border and used the same thread to free-motion quilt around the train appliqués. She finished by stipple quilting swirls of smoke around the train and crossing signals with thread to match the backgrounds.

3. Sew an appliquéd corner square to each short end of the bottom border strip; press. (This will be the strip with the appliqués reversed.) Sew the strip to the bottom of the quilt; press.

Finishing the Quilt

Refer to "Finishing" (page 9) as needed. For step-by-step instructions on quilt-finishing techniques (layering, basting, quilting, binding, and much more), please visit ShopMartingale.com/HowtoQuilt.

1. Layer the backing, batting, and quilt top; baste.

2. Hand or machine quilt as desired.

3. Use the 2½"-wide red strips to finish the edges of your quilt, incorporating a label and sleeve.

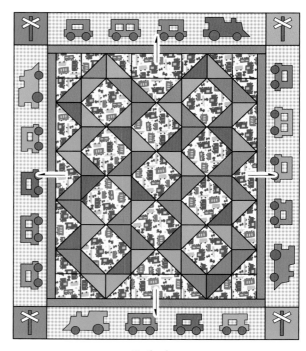

Quilt plan

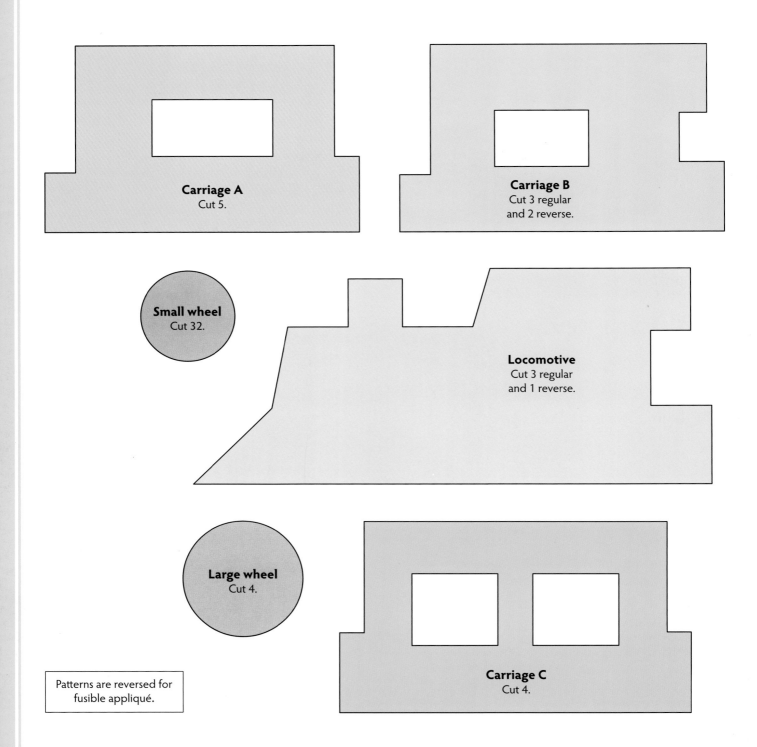

Carriage A
Cut 5.

Carriage B
Cut 3 regular
and 2 reverse.

Small wheel
Cut 32.

Locomotive
Cut 3 regular
and 1 reverse.

Large wheel
Cut 4.

Carriage C
Cut 4.

Patterns are reversed for
fusible appliqué.

grace's quilt

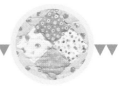

Quilt size: 31¾" x 44¼"
Finished block size: 6" x 6"
Number of blocks: 24
Fat-quarter friendly

▼▼▼

Chris stitched this sweet little quilt to welcome Grace, the daughter of her young friends James and May, into the world. A few clever shortcuts make its already-simple construction even simpler, and Chris's easy, yet elegant quilting adds to the quiet beauty of its classic design. Work it up in soft pastels as shown, or in any palette you choose; the 20"-long strips required make it perfect for those fat-quarter packs you've been longing to try.

Materials

Yardages are based on fabrics that measure 42" wide.

1⅓ yards *total* of assorted pastel prints for blocks and pieced border (darks)*
1⅛ yards *total* of assorted pastel prints on white backgrounds for blocks and pieced border (lights)*
⅝ yard of pastel-pink print for inner border and binding**
1½ yards of fabric for backing
36" x 49" piece of batting

Light and dark values are relative in this quilt; any pastel that's darker than a pastel on a white background can be used as a dark.

**The inner-border strips are cut at two different widths for this quilt. Although the variation is only ¼", to minimize the difference, we suggest you avoid a fabric that contrasts too strongly in value with the block-corner (dark) fabrics.*

Cutting

Measurements include ¼" seam allowance. Cut all strips on the crosswise grain (from selvage to selvage).

From the assorted pastel prints on white backgrounds (lights), cut a *total* of:
7 strips, 2⅝" x 20"
14 strips, 2¾" x 20"
8 squares, 2¾" x 2¾"

From the assorted pastel prints (darks), cut a *total* of:
7 strips, 2⅝" x 20"
24 pairs of matching squares, 4" x 4" (48 total); cut each square in half diagonally to make a total of 96 half-square triangles*
7 strips, 2¾" x 20"

From the pastel-pink print, cut:
2 strips, 1" x 42"
2 strips, 1¼" x 42"
5 strips, 2½" x 42"

These triangles are cut oversized; you'll trim them after completing the block.

Making the Blocks

1. With right sides together, sew a 2⅝"-wide assorted light strip and a 2⅝"-wide assorted dark strip together to make a strip set; press. Make a total of seven strip sets. Cut the strip sets into a total of 48 segments, 2⅝" wide.

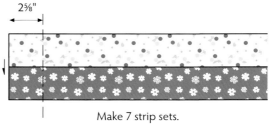

2⅝"

Make 7 strip sets.
Cut 48 segments.

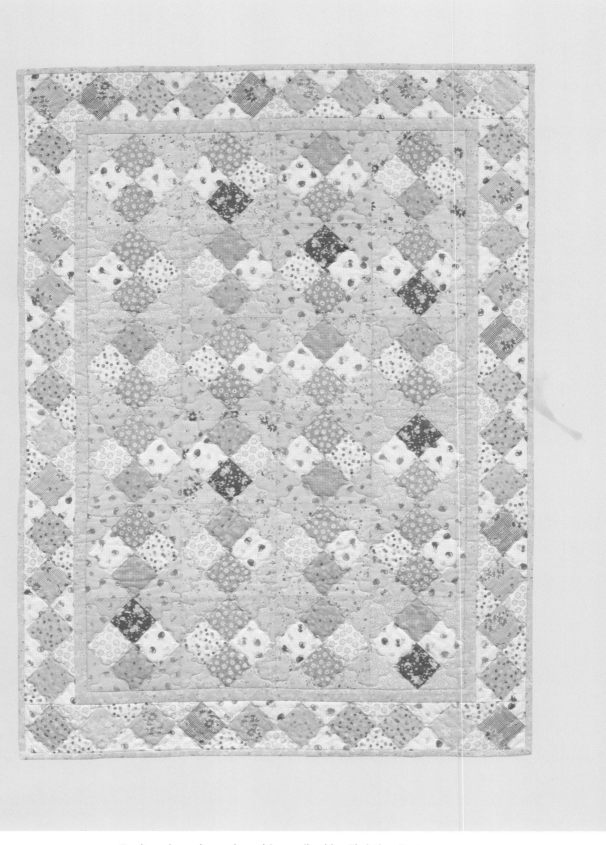

Designed, made, and machine quilted by Christine Porter

2. Sew two different segments from step 1 together as shown; press. Make a total of 24 scrappy units.

Make 24.

3. Sew matching half-square triangles to opposite sides of each unit from step 2; press. Sew half-square triangles cut from the same fabric to the remaining two sides; press. Make 24 blocks, trimming each block to measure 6½" x 6½".

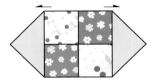

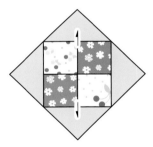

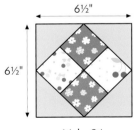

Make 24.

Assembling the Quilt

1. Arrange the blocks in six horizontal rows of four blocks each as shown in the quilt assembly diagram.

2. Sew the blocks together into horizontal rows; press. Sew the rows together; press.

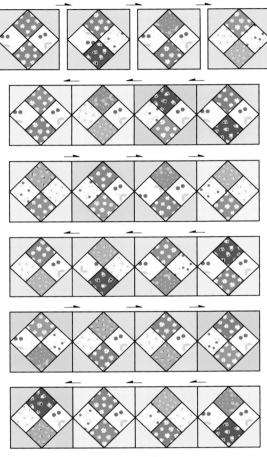

Quilt assembly

3. Measure the quilt through the center from top to bottom. Trim the two 1"-wide pastel-pink strips to this measurement. With right sides together, sew the strips to the sides of the quilt. Press the seam allowances toward the border.

4. Measure the quilt through the center from side to side, including the borders you've just added. Trim the two 1¼"-wide pastel-pink strips to this measurement, and sew them to the top and bottom of the quilt; press.

Making and Adding the Pieced Border

1. With right sides together, sew a 2¾"-wide assorted dark strip between two 2¾"-wide assorted light strips to make a strip set; press. Make a total of seven strip sets. Cut the strip sets into a total of 44 segments, 2¾" wide.

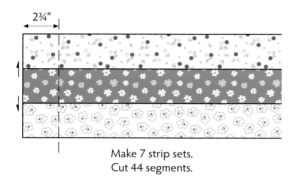

2¾"

Make 7 strip sets.
Cut 44 segments.

2. Sew 12 segments from step 1 together, staggering them as shown; press. Sew 2¾" assorted light squares to opposite ends to finish the unit as shown; press. Make two.

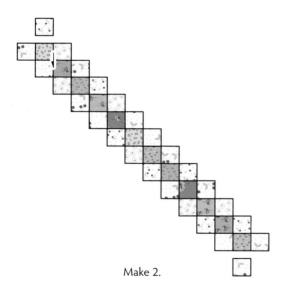

Make 2.

3. Carefully straighten the top, bottom, and side edges of each unit from step 2 by trimming ¼" from the outer corners of the dark squares as shown. Sew the trimmed units to the sides of the quilt, easing as necessary. Press the seam allowances toward the inner border.

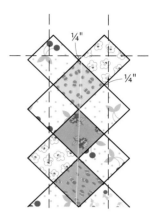

¼"

¼"

"Ease" into It

If you're joining two pieces, units, rows, or borders, and discover that one is a *little bit* longer than the other, try this simple solution. With right sides together, match and pin the midpoints, the ends, and any seams that must match *first*. Next, generously pin the gaps in between, distributing any excess fabric as evenly as possible. Finally—and this is key—sew with the larger piece on the bottom, against the throat plate of your machine. The action of the feed dogs helps take up the difference.

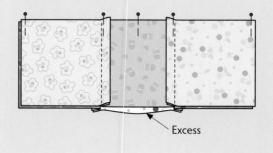

Excess

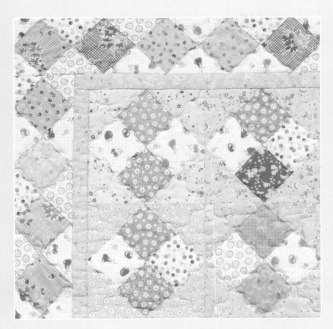

Detail of quilting on "Grace's Quilt"

SUGGESTIONS FOR QUILTING

Chris used clear monofilament to stitch in the ditch along the seams between the vertical and then the horizontal rows to anchor the quilt center.

Switching to a color-coordinated variegated thread, she quilted wavy lines right along the outside edges of the blocks in both directions. She used the same thread to quilt wavy lines through the center seams of each four-patch unit, continuing on from one block to the next for a secondary lattice pattern.

To complete the quilting, Chris returned to clear monofilament to quilt in the ditch on both sides of the inner border, and then returned to the variegated thread and wavy lines to quilt each diagonal seam in the pieced border.

4. Repeat steps 2 and 3, this time using 10 segments from step 1 to complete each unit. Sew the trimmed units to the top and bottom of the quilt, easing as necessary; press.

Finishing the Quilt

Refer to "Finishing" (page 9) as needed. For step-by-step instructions on quilt-finishing techniques (layering, basting, quilting, binding, and much more), please visit ShopMartingale.com/HowtoQuilt.

1. Layer the backing, batting, and quilt top; baste.
2. Hand or machine quilt as desired.
3. Use the 2½"-wide pastel-pink strips to finish the edges of your quilt, incorporating a label and sleeve.

Quilt plan

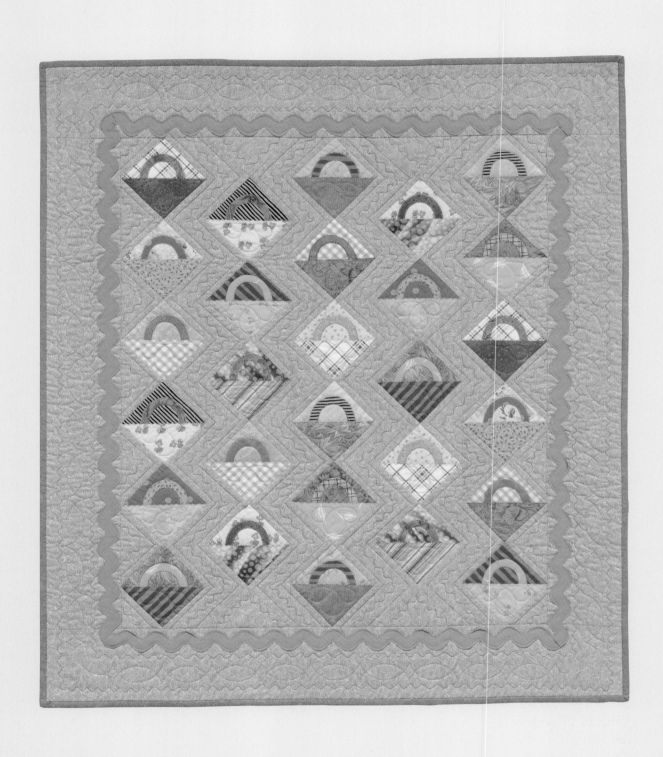

Designed and made by Darra Williamson; machine appliquéd and quilted by Christine Porter

a-tisket, a-tasket

Quilt size: 38⅝" x 44¼"
Finished block size: 4" x 4"
Number of blocks: 28
∗Charm-square friendly∗

▼▼▼

The time-honored Streak of Lightning setting teams up with a bright, contemporary color scheme; a new take on a familiar block; and some sassy embellishment in this fresh-and-fun cuddler. You'll love the streamlined, two-for-one block-piecing technique. And the setting? No problem! It may *look* advanced, but it's all done in rows! If you favor designs that give tradition a twist, you'll want to give this one a go.

Materials

Yardages are based on fabrics that measure 42" wide.

1½ yards of lime-green print for setting triangles and border
1 yard *total* of assorted pink, hot-pink, lime-green, and yellow-green scraps for baskets and handle appliqués*
½ yard of hot-pink print for binding
2⅜ yards of fabric for backing (horizontal seam)
43" x 49" piece of batting
3¾ yards of 1"-wide hot-pink rickrack
⅞ yard of 18"-wide lightweight fusible web
1⅛ yards of 13"-wide tear-away stabilizer
Threads in assorted pinks and greens for blanket-stitch appliqué
Pink sewing thread for securing the rickrack

You can substitute forty-two 5" charm squares for this yardage.

Cutting

Measurements include ¼" seam allowance. Cut all strips on the crosswise grain (from selvage to selvage). Use the appliqué pattern below.

From the assorted pink, hot-pink, lime-green, and yellow-green scraps, cut a total of:
42 squares, 5" x 5"

From the lime-green print, cut:
3 strips, 6⅞" x 42"; crosscut into 15 squares, 6⅞" x 6⅞". Cut each square into quarters diagonally to make a total of 60 quarter-square triangles. (You'll have 2 triangles left over.)
1 strip, 3¾" x 42"; crosscut into 6 squares, 3¾" x 3¾". Cut each square in half diagonally to make a total of 12 half-square triangles.
4 strips, 5½" x 42"

From the hot-pink print, cut:
5 strips, 2½" x 42"

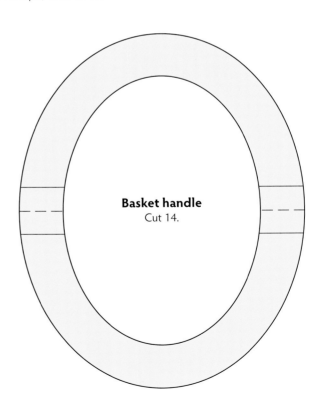

Basket handle
Cut 14.

Making the Blocks

Refer to "Adding Appliqués" (page 8) for help as needed.

1. Sort the assorted 5" pink, hot-pink, lime-green, and yellow-green squares into 14 groups of three squares each, designating one for the basket bottom, one for the handle appliqué, and one for the background.

2. Working with one group of squares at a time, follow the manufacturer's instructions for the fusible web to prepare the 5" handle square for fusing.

3. Use the pattern on page 47 to make a template. Use the template to trace and cut a handle from the prepared handle square.

4. Fold the 5" background square into quarters diagonally; finger-press lightly. This marks the center of the background square to assist you with appliqué placement.

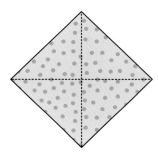

5. Center the handle appliqué on the 5" background square as shown. Adhere the appliqué to the block.

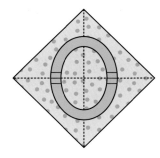

6. Secure the appliqué to the background square using a machine or hand blanket stitch.

7. Draw a diagonal line from corner to corner on the wrong side of the appliquéd background block. This will be your cutting line. Draw a line ¼" from the diagonal line on both sides. These lines will be your sewing lines.

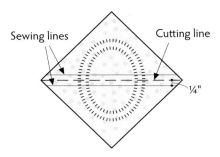

Sewing lines   Cutting line   ¼"

8. Place the marked appliquéd background square and the 5" basket-bottom square right sides together. Sew directly on the two outermost lines. Cut the unit apart on the center diagonal line; press. You now have two identical Basket blocks. Trim the blocks, if necessary, to measure 4½" x 4½".

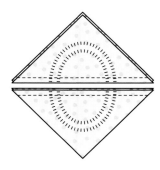

9. Repeat steps 2–8 to make a total of 28 blocks.

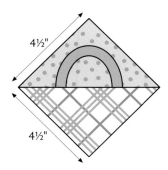

4½"

4½"

Make 28.

Assembling the Quilt

1. Arrange the blocks, the quarter-square (side) setting triangles, and the half-square (corner) setting triangles in five vertical rows as shown in the quilt assembly diagram.

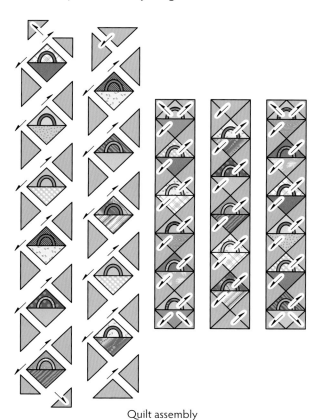

Quilt assembly

2. Working one row at a time, sew each block between two setting triangles as shown; press. In some cases you'll be sewing two side setting triangles to the block, and sometimes you'll be sewing a side setting triangle and a corner setting triangle.

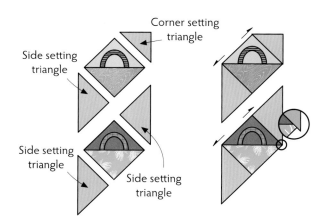

3. Sew together the units from step 2; press.

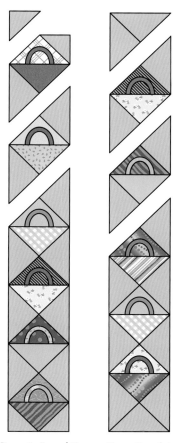

Rows 1, 3, and 5   Rows 2 and 4

4. Repeat steps 2 and 3 to piece a total of five vertical rows as shown in the quilt assembly diagram. Finish rows 1, 3, and 5 by adding the remaining corner setting triangles; press. For rows 2 and 4, sew together the pairs of side setting triangles remaining at the top and bottom of the rows; press. Sew the paired triangles to the row corners; press.

5. If necessary, carefully straighten the edges of each row by trimming ¼" from the outer corners of the blocks. Square the row corners.

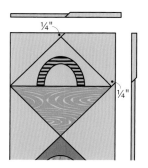

6. Starting with row 1, measure and mark the center point of each side setting triangle, and then return it to its place in the quilt layout. Repeat for rows 2–5.

7. Sew the rows together, carefully matching the corners of the staggered blocks with the guide marks you made in step 6; press.

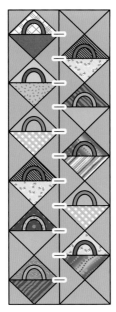

Tick marks are for illustration only.

Adding the Border

1. Measure the quilt through the center from top to bottom. Trim two 5½"-wide lime-green strips to this measurement. With right sides together, sew the strips to the sides of the quilt. Press the seam allowances toward the border.

2. Measure the quilt through the center from side to side, including the borders you've just added. Trim the remaining two 5½"-wide lime-green strips to this measurement and sew them to the top and bottom of the quilt; press.

Finishing the Quilt

Refer to "Finishing" (page 9) as needed. For step-by-step instructions on quilt-finishing techniques (layering, basting, quilting, binding, and much more), please visit ShopMartingale.com/HowtoQuilt.

1. Lay out the backing so the seam runs horizontally and add the batting and quilt top; baste.

2. Hand or machine quilt the center of the quilt as desired; stop when you reach the outer border.

Detail of quilting on "A-Tisket, A-Tasket"

SUGGESTIONS FOR QUILTING

Chris began by using clear monofilament to quilt in the ditch along all the diagonal seams. Once the quilt was anchored, she used matching thread to stitch right around the edges of the handle appliqués. She then used green or dark-pink thread to free-motion quilt a three-leaf clover motif in the bottom half of each basket.

To emphasize the zigzag setting, Chris stitched approximately ⅜" from the outside edges of the blocks with dark-pink thread, and then free-motion quilted wavy lines between the rows of stitching and in the side and corner setting triangles. The border seam was quilted in the ditch with clear monofilament.

Once the rickrack was added, Chris used dark-pink thread to finish the outer border with a free-motion half-circle-and-diamond pattern, outlining the pattern on both sides with more wavy-line stitching.

3. Referring to the quilt photo on page 46 and the detail photo above, place the hot-pink rickrack on the border, all around the perimeter of the quilt center, so that the trim just touches the border seam. Fold the rickrack at each corner as necessary to achieve a smooth turn. Trim the excess rickrack, leaving an overlap of approximately 1". Pin generously to secure the rickrack to the quilt. Using matching pink thread, sew down both sides of the rickrack.

4. Quilt the outer border as desired.

5. Use the 2½"-wide hot-pink strips to finish the edges of your quilt, incorporating a label and sleeve.

Quilt plan

Designed and made by Darra Williamson; machine quilted by Christine Porter

it takes a village

Quilt size: 32½" x 38½"
Finished block size:
House and Tree: 4" x 6"
Picket Fence: 4" x 6¼"
Picket Fence corner: 4" x 4"
Total number of blocks: 36
House: 20 | Tree: 10
Picket Fence: 4
Picket Fence corner: 2
⁂Charm-square friendly⁂
⁂Precut-strip friendly⁂

"It takes a village to raise a child." Although the source of this oft-heard adage has never been identified—it's thought to be based on an African proverb—its truth is undisputed. Just ask any new mother! Our cozy, picket-fenced village goes together in a snap using quick cutting and piecing techniques, and with a minimum of points to match. The treetops and houses make great use of those colorful charm squares and precut strips you've been hoarding. Don't miss the opportunity to add a few personal touches . . . perhaps a family pet in a doorway or two?

Materials

Yardages are based on fabrics that measure 42" wide.

⅞ yard *total* of assorted peach, yellow, turquoise, red, and green prints for House blocks*
⅝ yard of medium green-striped fabric for Picket Fence and Picket Fence corner blocks, inner border, and binding

⅝ yard of medium-green batik for Picket Fence and Picket Fence corner blocks, and outer border
½ yard of light-aqua tone-on-tone print for House and Tree block backgrounds
¼ yard *total* of assorted light- and medium-green prints for Tree blocks**
¼ yard of white pin-dot print for Picket Fence and Picket Fence corner blocks
⅛ yard of golden-brown tone-on-tone print for Tree blocks
1⅜ yards of fabric for backing
39" x 45" piece of batting

*You can substitute assorted 2½"-wide precut strips for this yardage. Trim the strips to the widths specified in "Cutting".

**You can substitute ten 5" charm squares (trimmed to 4½") for this yardage.

Cutting

Measurements include ¼" seam allowance. Cut all strips on the crosswise grain (from selvage to selvage).

From the light-aqua tone-on-tone print, cut:
5 strips, 2½" x 42"; crosscut 3 strips into 40 squares, 2½" x 2½"
2 strips, 1½" x 42"; crosscut into 40 squares, 1½" x 1½"
2 strips, 2" x 42"

From the assorted peach, yellow, turquoise, red, and green prints, cut a *total* of:
20 rectangles, 2" x 3¼" (fabric B)
20 rectangles, 2½" x 4½" (fabric C)
Then cut the following matching pieces for *each* of the 20 House blocks:
2 rectangles, 1¾" x 3¼" (fabric A)
1 rectangle, 1¾" x 4½" (fabric A)

From the golden-brown tone-on-tone print, cut:
1 strip, 1½" x 42"

Continued on page 54

From the assorted light- and medium-green prints, cut a *total* of:

10 squares, 4½" x 4½"

From the white pin-dot print, cut:

2 strips, 1½" x 42"; crosscut into 16 rectangles, 1½" x 4½"

3 strips, 1¼" x 42"; crosscut *1* strip into:
    2 squares, 1¼" x 1¼"
    2 rectangles, 1¼" x 2"
    2 rectangles, 1¼" x 3"
    2 rectangles, 1¼" x 3¾"

From the medium green-striped fabric, cut:

4 strips, 1¼" x 42"; crosscut *3* strips into:
    2 strips, 1¼" x 19"
    2 strips, 1¼" x 24¼"
    2 squares, 1¼" x 1¼"

5 strips, 2½" x 42"

From the medium-green batik, cut:

1 strip, 1" x 42"; crosscut into 32 squares, 1" x 1"

2 strips, 1¼" x 42"; crosscut *1* strip into:
    2 rectangles, 1¼" x 3¾"
    2 rectangles, 1¼" x 4½"

2 strips, 1½" x 42"; crosscut *1* strip into:
    2 rectangles, 1½" x 2"
    2 rectangles, 1½" x 3"

3 strips, 3¾" x 42"; crosscut into:
    2 strips, 3¾" x 19"
    2 strips, 3¾" x 24¼"
    2 rectangles, 3¾" x 4½"

Making the House Blocks

1. Sew a 2" x 3¼" fabric B rectangle between two matching 1¾" x 3¼" fabric A rectangles; press.

2. Sew a matching 1¾" x 4½" fabric A rectangle to the top of the unit from step 1; press.

3. Referring to "Sew-and-Flip Technique" (page 7), sew a 2½" light-aqua square to each end of a 2½" x 4½" fabric C rectangle; trim and press.

4. Sew the unit from step 3 to the top edge of the unit from step 2; press.

5. Repeat steps 1–4 to make a total of 20 House blocks.

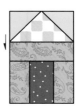

Make 20.

Making the Tree Blocks

1. Using the sew-and-flip technique, sew 1½" light-aqua squares to the four corners of a 4½" assorted green square; trim and press. Make 10.

Make 10.

2. With right sides together, sew the 1½"-wide brown strip between two 2"-wide light-aqua strips along their long edges to make a strip

set; press. Cut the strip set into a total of 10 segments, 2½" wide.

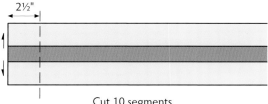

Cut 10 segments.

3. Sew a unit from step 1 to a segment from step 2; press. Make 10.

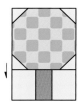

Make 10.

Assembling the Quilt

1. Arrange four House and two Tree blocks *each* in five horizontal rows as shown in the quilt assembly diagram.

2. Sew the blocks together in horizontal rows; press. Sew the rows together; press.

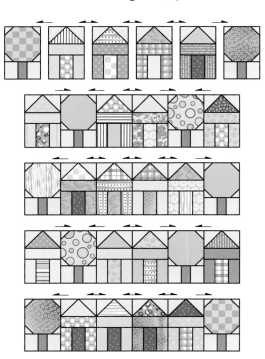

Quilt assembly

Re-press Reminder

Before sewing the House blocks together, re-press the horizontal seam allowances on alternate blocks in the opposite direction. When you pin the two blocks together, the seams will nest for a nice, neat match.

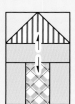 

Assembling the Picket Fence Blocks

1. Using the sew-and-flip technique, sew 1" medium-green batik squares to each corner of one end of a 1½" x 4½" white rectangle; press. Make 16.

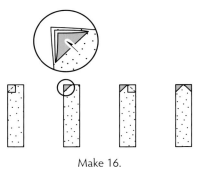

Make 16.

When *Not* to Trim

When you're using the sew-and-flip technique, and the squares you're sewing to the larger unit are cut 1" or smaller, press toward the smaller square as usual, but do not trim the excess fabric to leave a ¼" seam allowance. The extra fabric helps to stabilize the tiny triangles.

2. Arrange a 1¼" x 42" medium-green batik strip, a 1¼" x 42" white strip, a 1½" x 42" medium-green batik strip, a 1¼" x 42" white strip, and a 1¼" x 42" medium green-striped strip as shown. With right sides together, sew the strips together along their long edges to make a strip set; press. Cut the strip set into a total of 12 segments, 1¼" wide.

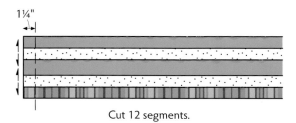

Cut 12 segments.

3. Arrange four units from step 1 and three segments from step 2, alternating them as shown. Sew the units and segments together; press. Make four.

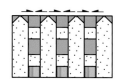

Make 4.

Assembling the Picket Fence Corner Blocks

1. Sew a 1¼" white square to the left edge of a 1¼" medium green-striped square; press. Sew a 1¼" x 2" white rectangle to the top of the unit; press.

2. Sew a 1½" x 2" medium-green batik rectangle to the left edge of the unit from step 1; press. Sew a 1½" x 3" medium-green batik rectangle to the top of the unit; press.

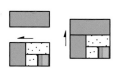

3. Sew a 1¼" x 3" white rectangle to the left edge of the unit from step 2; press. Sew a 1¼" x 3¾" white rectangle to the top of the unit; press.

4. Sew a 1¼" x 3¾" medium-green batik rectangle to the left edge of the unit from step 3; press. Sew a 1¼" x 4½" medium-green batik rectangle to the top of the unit; press.

5. Repeat steps 1–4 for a second corner block.

Make 2.

Adding the Borders

1. With right sides together, sew a 1¼" x 24¼" medium green-striped strip and a 3¾" x 24¼" medium-green batik strip together along their long edges. Press the seam allowances toward the wider strip. Make two.

2. Sew a Picket Fence block to one end of each unit from step 1 as shown; press.

Make 2.

3. Referring to the quilt plan (opposite), sew the border units from step 2 to the sides of the quilt top. Press the seam allowances toward the border units.

4. With right sides together, sew a 1¼" x 19" medium green-striped strip and a 3¾" x 19" medium-green batik strip together along their long edges. Press the seam allowances toward the wider strip. Make two.

Detail of quilting on "It Takes a Village"

SUGGESTIONS FOR QUILTING

Chris began by quilting in the ditch around all the trees and houses using clear monofilament. With a bit of planning, this can be done in long, continuous lines of stitching, eliminating the need for lots of stops and starts. She used the same transparent thread to quilt in the ditch on both sides of the inner border and around the pickets and fence posts.

Once the quilt was stabilized, Chris indulged her creative side, using matching threads to free-motion quilt a variety of motifs on the treetops and houses. She allowed the fabrics to suggest many of her choices, incorporating leaf fronds, flowers, door panels, roof tiles, and so on. In her words, "I just had fun!"

For the finishing touch, Chris used matching green thread to quilt a simple, continuous cable design in the outer border.

5. Arrange a Picket Fence corner block, a Picket Fence block, a border unit from step 4, and a 3¾" x 4½" medium-green batik rectangle as shown. Sew the blocks, border unit, and rectangle together; press. Make two.

Make 2.

6. Referring to the quilt plan, sew the border units from step 5 to the top and bottom of the quilt top; press.

Finishing the Quilt

Refer to "Finishing" (page 9) as needed. For step-by-step instructions on quilt-finishing techniques (layering, basting, quilting, binding, and much more), please visit ShopMartingale.com/HowtoQuilt.

1. Layer the backing, batting, and quilt top; baste.

2. Hand or machine quilt as desired.

3. Use the 2½"-wide medium green-striped strips to finish the edges of your quilt, incorporating a label and sleeve.

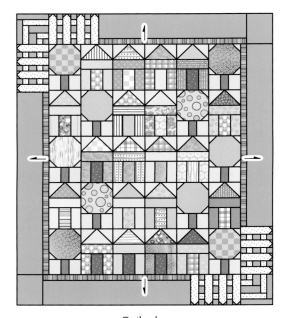

Quilt plan

Designed, made, and machine quilted by Christine Porter

you are my sunshine

Quilt size: 43" x 54½"
Finished diamond size:
6½" (per side)

▼▼▼

Like the chorus of the familiar song from which it draws its name, this sunny quilt will bring a warm, cheerful glow—and lots of smiles—to *any* nursery. The center of the quilt is pieced entirely from diamonds that are trimmed and squared before the borders are added—no odd half-diamond filler pieces to fuss with. The appliqués are simple, and a lattice of rickrack adds charm and texture. Why not make one for your own special ray of sunshine?

Materials

Yardages are based on fabrics that measure 42" wide. Fat quarters measure approximately 18" x 21".

1⅔ yards of light multicolored print for diamonds, background, and outer border (A)
1 yard of medium-blue dotted print for diamonds, inner border, and binding (B)
¼ yard *each* of medium-green print (C), yellow print (D), light-blue print (E), medium-green tone-on-tone dotted print (F), *and* medium-orange tone-on-tone print (G) for diamonds
Fat quarter of yellow dotted print for circle appliqués
2⅝ yards of fabric for backing (horizontal seam)
47" x 59" piece of batting
⅓ yard of 18"-wide lightweight fusible web
½ yard of 13"-wide tear-away stabilizer
15¾ yards of ½"-wide white-with-yellow rickrack
Non-permanent marker
Blue thread for embroidery
Yellow thread for satin-stitch appliqué
Matching thread for stitching rickrack

Cutting

Measurements include ¼" seam allowance. Cut all strips on the crosswise grain (from selvage to selvage). Use the appliqué pattern on page 63.

From the light multicolored print (A), cut:
5 strips, 6⅛" x 42"
5 strips, 4½" x 42"

From the medium-blue dotted print (B), cut:
1 strip, 6⅛" x 42"
5 strips, 1½" x 42"
6 strips, 2½" x 42"

From the medium-green (C), yellow (D), light-blue (E), medium-green tone-on-tone dotted (F), and medium-orange tone-on-tone (G) prints, cut:
1 strip *each*, 6⅛" x 42" (5 total)

From the yellow dotted print, cut:
8 circle appliqués

Going 'Round in Circles

Use a small (e.g., 18 mm) rotary cutter to cut the appliqués. The smaller size makes it easier to negotiate the curved edges of the circles. If you prefer, cut the circle appliqués with small, curved scissors. (See "Curves Ahead!" on page 8.)

Cutting Diamonds from Strips

You need to cut a total of 40 diamonds from the assorted 6⅛"-wide fabric (A–G) strips: 21 diamonds from A; five diamonds each from B, C, D, E, and G; and 4 diamonds from F.

Diamonds Rule!

Chris has designed a diamond-shaped, non-slip acrylic ruler that is the exact size of the diamond required for this quilt, including the seam allowance. No marking is necessary; the ruler makes cutting the diamonds a snap (see "Resources" on page 11).

Trim the edge of the 6⅛" strip as described in step 1 below. Align the angled edge of the diamond ruler with the strip's newly angled edge. Cut along the opposite edge of the ruler to separate the diamond from the strip. Repeat until you've cut the required number of diamonds from each fabric, and then proceed to step 5. Use the blunted ends of the diamond ruler to blunt the ends of the fabric diamonds.

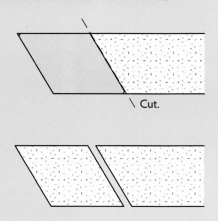

1. Place a 6⅛"-wide fabric A strip right side up on your cutting board. Align the 60° marking on your rotary ruler with the bottom edge of the strip as shown; trim.

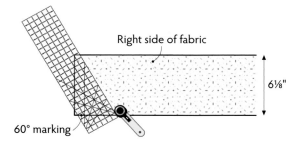

2. Measure 7" from the angled cut along the top and bottom edges of the strip; mark the measurements with a non-permanent marker. Place your rotary ruler on the strip, connecting the marks and aligning the 60° marking on the ruler with the bottom edge of the strip as shown.

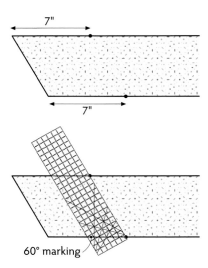

3. Using your rotary cutter and ruler, cut the diamond shape from the strip. Continue marking and cutting until you have cut 21 diamonds from the fabric A strips.

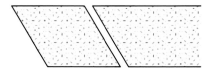

4. Repeat steps 2 and 3 to cut the required number of diamonds from fabrics B–G. After every few cuts, use the 60° marking on your rotary ruler to make certain that you're maintaining a 60° angle with each cut. If not, re-trim the fabric edge to reestablish the angle.

5. Use your rotary ruler and cutter to blunt the two skinny points on each diamond as shown. This makes it easier to match up the diamonds when sewing them together into rows.

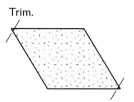

Appliquéing the Blocks

You'll appliqué a yellow circle to eight of the diamonds: three light multicolored diamonds (A) and the five medium-blue dotted diamonds (B).

1. Fold an A diamond into quarters as shown; finger-press lightly. This marks the center of the diamond to assist you with appliqué placement. Repeat with a yellow circle.

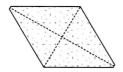

2. Referring to the appliqué pattern on page 63, use a non-permanent marker to draw the eyes and mouth on the yellow circle. Matching the folds, center the marked appliqué on the diamond as shown.

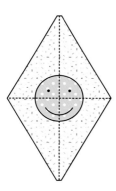

3. Following the manufacturer's instructions for the fusible web, adhere the appliqué to the diamond.

4. Secure the appliqué to the diamond using a machine satin stitch and bright yellow thread. Use blue thread to satin stitch the mouth. If the decorative stitches on your machine include an eyelet stitch, you can use it to create the eyes with blue thread. See "Stitching Options" at right for additional possibilities.

5. Repeat steps 1–4 to appliqué and embroider the two remaining A diamonds and the five B diamonds.

Stitching Options

If you prefer, use a machine or hand blanket stitch to secure the appliqués to the diamonds, a hand or machine straight stitch to embroider the mouth, and large French knots to make the eyes.

Assembling the Quilt

Quilting can cause the quilt to shrink slightly, so wait until the center of the quilt is quilted before adding the rickrack. This eliminates puckering in the finished quilt, and makes quilting easier, too.

1. Arrange the diamonds as shown in the quilt assembly diagram, placing light multicolored diamonds (A) all around the outside edges.

2. Sew the diamonds together into diagonal rows; press.

3. Sew the rows together, taking care to match the diamond points; press.

Quilt assembly

4. Carefully straighten the edges of the quilt top by trimming a generous ¼" from the outer points of the diamonds. Square the quilt corners.

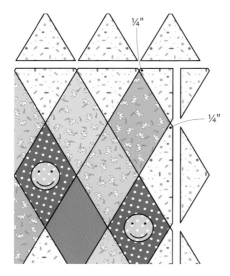

Adding the Borders

1. Sew the 1½"-wide medium-blue dotted strips together end to end using diagonal seams to make one long strip. Measure the quilt through the center from top to bottom, and cut two 1½"-wide medium-blue dotted strips to this measurement. With right sides together, sew the strips to the sides of the quilt. Press the seam allowances toward the border.

2. Measure the quilt through the center from side to side, including the borders you've just added. From the remaining 1½"-wide medium-blue dotted strip, cut two strips to this measurement and sew them to the top and bottom of the quilt; press.

3. Sew the 4½"-wide light multicolored strips together end to end using diagonal seams to make one long strip. Repeat steps 1 and 2 to measure, cut, and sew the strips to the sides, top, and bottom of the quilt. Press the seam allowances toward the newly added border.

Finishing the Quilt

Refer to "Finishing" (page 9) as needed. For step-by-step instructions on quilt-finishing techniques (layering, basting, quilting, binding, and much more), please visit ShopMartingale.com/ HowtoQuilt.

1. Lay out the backing so the seam runs horizontally and add the batting and quilt top; baste.

2. Hand or machine quilt the center area of the quilt as desired. Stop when you reach the inner border. Do not quilt the seam that joins the quilt center and the inner border.

3. Working in one direction at a time, measure each diagonal seam in the quilt center. Cut a piece of ½"-wide rickrack to the measurement of each seam, *plus a generous ½"* for tucking in.

4. Set your machine for a slightly longer straight stitch than you typically use for piecing. Allowing a generous ¼" overhang on each end, place the appropriate length of rickrack over one long diagonal seam near the center of the quilt top. Using matching thread, sew down the center of the rickrack to attach it to the quilt, leaving the overhanging ends free. Working from the center outward, cover and stitch the rickrack to all the diagonal seams running in one direction first, and then repeat to cover all the remaining diagonal seams.

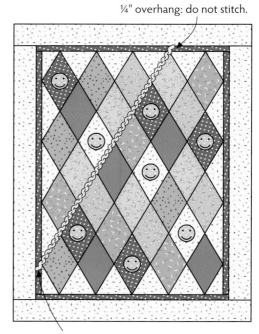

¼" overhang: do not stitch.

¼" overhang: do not stitch.

5. Carefully open the seam approximately 1" between the quilt center and the inner border as needed to insert the rickrack tails; pin. Use clear monofilament to quilt in the ditch

Detail of quilting on "You Are My Sunshine"

SUGGESTIONS FOR QUILTING

Chris took advantage of the shapes in the quilt to design her quilting strategy. She began by using yellow variegated thread to quilt diagonal lines approximately ½" from both sides of each diagonal seam. This gives you the added bonus of providing guidelines for keeping the rickrack straight as you sew it to the quilt.

Changing to clear monofilament, Chris then free-motion quilted in the ditch around the circle appliqués. She centered and traced the template for the circle appliqué in each appliqué-free diamond, and quilted with thread to match the diamond. She did the same to quilt half circles in the setting diamonds around the outer edges of the quilt center.

Once the rickrack had been added and tucked into the border seam, Chris used invisible thread to quilt in the ditch on both inner-border seams. She finished by quilting the outer border with a diamond motif in yellow variegated thread, filling in the background with continuous squiggles and circles.

between the quilt center and the inner border to secure the tails and close the open areas of the seam. Finish by quilting the outer border.

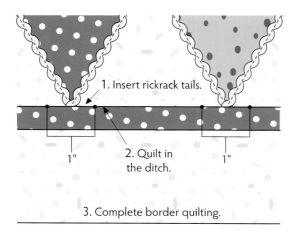

1. Insert rickrack tails.

1"

2. Quilt in the ditch.

1"

3. Complete border quilting.

6. Use the 2½"-wide medium-blue dotted strips to finish the edges of your quilt, incorporating a label and sleeve.

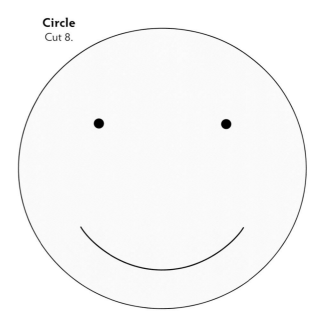

Circle
Cut 8.

Designed and made by Darra Williamson; machine quilted by Christine Porter

little sailor

Quilt size: 50" x 60"
Finished block sizes:
Sailboat: 8" x 6" | Waves: 8" x 4"
Total number of blocks:
Sailboat: 25 | Waves: 25
Charm-square friendly
Precut-strip friendly

▼▼▼

This jaunty, nautical-themed quilt is the largest in the book: perfect for cuddling your little sailor now, and for later transitioning nicely to a coverlet for the big-boy/big-girl bed to come. It's also a natural for charm squares and precut strips, or for using up other small bits from your stash. Believe it or not, Darra didn't cut a *single* triangle to make this quilt; the super-simple sew-and-flip technique was used throughout. The forecast couldn't be more favorable for a smooth sail!

Materials

Yardages are based on fabrics that measure 42" wide.

1½ yards *total* of assorted light and medium brightly colored prints for Sailboat blocks*

1⅛ yards *total* of assorted medium and dark brightly colored prints for Sailboat blocks*

1⅛ yards *total* of assorted dark blue and blue-green prints for Wave blocks**

1⅛ yards *total* of assorted light blue and blue-green prints for Wave blocks**

1 yard of blue-green print for outer border

½ yard of multicolored plaid fabric for binding

3⅛ yards of fabric for backing (horizontal seam)

54" x 64" piece of batting

5¾ yards of ½"-wide white-with-yellow rickrack

Matching thread for stitching rickrack

*You can substitute twenty-five 5" charm squares (trimmed to 4½"), and 2½"-wide precut strips for these yardages.

**You can substitute 2½"-wide precut strips for these yardages.

Cutting

Measurements include ¼" seam allowances. Cut all strips on the crosswise grain (from selvage to selvage).

From the assorted medium and dark brightly colored prints, cut a *total* of:
25 squares, 4½" x 4½"
25 rectangles, 2½" x 8½"

From the assorted light and medium brightly colored prints, cut a *total* of 25 matching sets of the following:
1 square, 4½" x 4½"
2 rectangles, 2½" x 4½"
2 squares, 2½" x 2½"

From the assorted dark blue and blue-green prints, cut a *total* of:
50 rectangles, 2½" x 4½"
100 squares, 2½" x 2½"

From the assorted light blue and blue-green prints, cut a *total* of:
50 rectangles, 2½" x 4½"
100 squares, 2½" x 2½"

From the blue-green print for outer border, cut:
6 strips, 5¼" x 42"

From the multicolored plaid fabric, cut:
6 strips, 2½" x 42"

Making the Sailboat Blocks

1. Draw a diagonal line from corner to corner on the wrong side of a 4½" background square. Place the marked square right sides together with a 4½" assorted print square. Sew directly on the marked line. Trim the seam allowances to ¼"; press.

2. Sew the unit from step 1 between two matching 2½" x 4½" background rectangles; press.

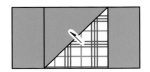

3. Referring to "Sew-and-Flip Technique" (page 7), sew matching 2½" background squares to both ends of a 2½" x 8½" assorted print rectangle; trim and press.

4. Sew the units from steps 2 and 3 together; press. Repeat steps 1–4 to make a total of 25 Sailboat blocks.

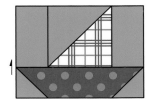

Make 25.

Changing Winds

If you'd like, reverse the direction of some of the Sailboat blocks for a whimsical effect. We reversed three blocks. Just turn the unit from step 1 a quarter turn clockwise before sewing on the two 2½" x 4½" background rectangles. The rest of the assembly process remains the same.

Making the Wave Blocks

1. Using the sew-and-flip technique, sew a 2½" light blue or blue-green square to one end of a 2½" x 4½" dark blue or blue-green rectangle; trim and press. Sew a different 2½" light blue or blue-green square to the other end of the rectangle; trim and press. Make two.

Make 2.

2. Sew the two units from step 1 together side by side; press.

3. Sew a 2½" dark blue or blue-green square to one end of a 2½" x 4½" light blue or blue-green rectangle; trim and press. Sew a different 2½" dark blue or blue-green square to the other end of the rectangle; trim and press. Make two, and sew them side by side; press.

4. Sew the units from steps 2 and 3 together as shown; press.

5. Repeat steps 1–4 to make a total of 25 Wave blocks.

Make 25.

Assembling the Quilt

1. Arrange five Sailboat and five Wave blocks *each* in five vertical rows, alternating the Sailboat and Wave blocks as shown in the quilt assembly diagram.

2. Sew the blocks together into vertical rows; press. Sew the rows together; press.

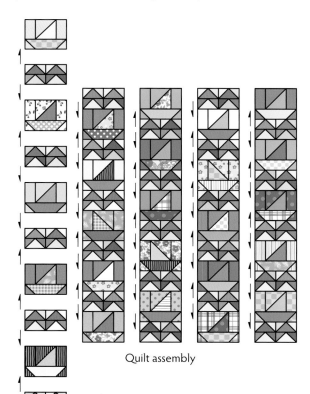

Quilt assembly

Dealing with Directional Prints

If you cut the small squares from a directional print, it's easy to have the prints running in all directions.

Sometimes this isn't a problem, but if it is, remember this little tip: When you place the small, directional square right sides together on the larger piece, place it so the direction of the print runs *opposite* the way you want it to run in the finished unit. When you've sewn, trimmed, and pressed—presto!

3. Sew the 5¼"-wide blue-green strips together end to end using diagonal seams to make one long strip. Measure the quilt through the center from top to bottom, and cut two 5¼"-wide blue-green strips to this measurement. With right sides together, sew the strips to the sides of the quilt. Press the seam allowances toward the border.

4. Measure the quilt through the center from side to side, including the borders you've just added. From the remaining 5¼"-wide blue-green strip, cut two strips to this measurement and sew them to the top and bottom of the quilt; press.

Detail of quilting on "Little Sailor"

SUGGESTIONS FOR QUILTING

Chris used a wavy line and brightly colored variegated thread to stitch around the outer edges of the Sailboat blocks, sails, and the boat bottoms. She switched to a variegated blue thread to stitch wavy lines along the outer edges of the wave triangles, and used clear monofilament to stitch in the ditch in the seam between the quilt center and the outer border.

Using thread to match the various fabrics, Chris free-motion quilted the sky around the sails and in the boat bottoms in designs influenced by the various fabrics. Once the rickrack was added, she placed the finishing touches by quilting a smaller version of the sailboat shape in the outer border with bright-yellow thread, filling in the background with stipple quilting in turquoise thread.

Finishing the Quilt

Refer to "Finishing" (page 9) as needed. For step-by-step instructions on quilt-finishing techniques (layering, basting, quilting, binding, and much more), please visit ShopMartingale.com/HowtoQuilt.

1. Lay out the backing so the seam runs horizontally and add the batting and quilt top; baste.

2. Hand or machine quilt the center of the quilt as desired; stop when you reach the outer border.

3. Referring to the photo on page 64, place the rickrack on the border, all around the perimeter of the quilt center, directly over the border seam. Fold the rickrack at each corner as necessary to achieve a smooth turn. Trim the excess rickrack, leaving an overlap of approximately 1". Pin generously to secure the rickrack to the quilt. Using matching thread, sew down the center of the rickrack to secure it to the quilt.

4. Quilt the outer border as desired.

5. Use the 2½"-wide multicolored plaid strips to finish your quilt, incorporating a label and sleeve.

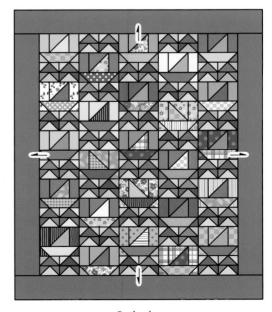

Quilt plan

alphabet soup

Here's a quilt that does double duty in the nursery. Not only is it perfect for snuggling, but—as the child grows—the design becomes a terrific tool for teaching your little cutie colors and letters, as well as basic counting skills. The playfully tilted blocks, multicolored inner border, and scrappy binding boost visual appeal, while the fused, machine-stitched appliqués make construction as easy as . . . well, 1, 2, 3!

Materials

Yardages are based on fabrics that measure 42" wide.

2½ yards *total* of assorted bright blue, turquoise, green, yellow, red, and orange prints for Alphabet blocks, inner border, and binding*

¾ yard of white polka-dot print for Number blocks and outer border

⅝ yard *total* of assorted bright blue, turquoise, green, yellow, red, and orange dotted prints for alphabet and number appliqués

2½ yards of fabric for backing (horizontal seam)

43" x 49" piece of batting

1⅜ yards of 18"-wide lightweight fusible web

2⅛ yards of 13"-wide tear-away stabilizer

Tracing paper

Fine-tip permanent marking pen

6½" x 6½" square ruler

½"- to ⅝"-wide clear tape, suitable for marking

You can substitute twenty-six 5" charm squares, and assorted 2½"-wide precut strips for these yardages.

Cutting

Measurements include ¼" seam allowance. Cut all strips on the crosswise grain (from selvage to selvage). Use the appliqué patterns on pages 76–79.

From the assorted bright prints, cut a *total* of:
26 squares, 5" x 5"
26 strips, 2" x 30"; crosscut *each* strip into 4 strips, 2" x 7"*

From one *each* of the assorted bright yellow and turquoise prints, cut:
1 strip, 1½" x 37½" (2 total)

From one *each* of the assorted bright orange and green prints, cut:
1 strip, 1½" x 31½" (2 total)

From the leftover assorted bright blue, turquoise, green, yellow, red, and orange prints, cut:
2½"-wide strips to total approximately 185"

From the white polka-dot print, cut:
1 strip, 6½" x 42"; crosscut into 4 squares, 6½" x 6½"
4 strips, 3¾" x 42"

From the assorted bright dotted prints, cut:
1 *each* of alphabet appliqués A–Z**
1 *each* of number appliqués 1–4

If you use 2½"-wide precut strips, you do not need to trim them down to 2"; trimming will be accomplished when the blocks are squared to size.

**You may wish to wait until the background blocks are made and trimmed before cutting the appliqués so that you can choose colors for letters that contrast with the block backgrounds.*

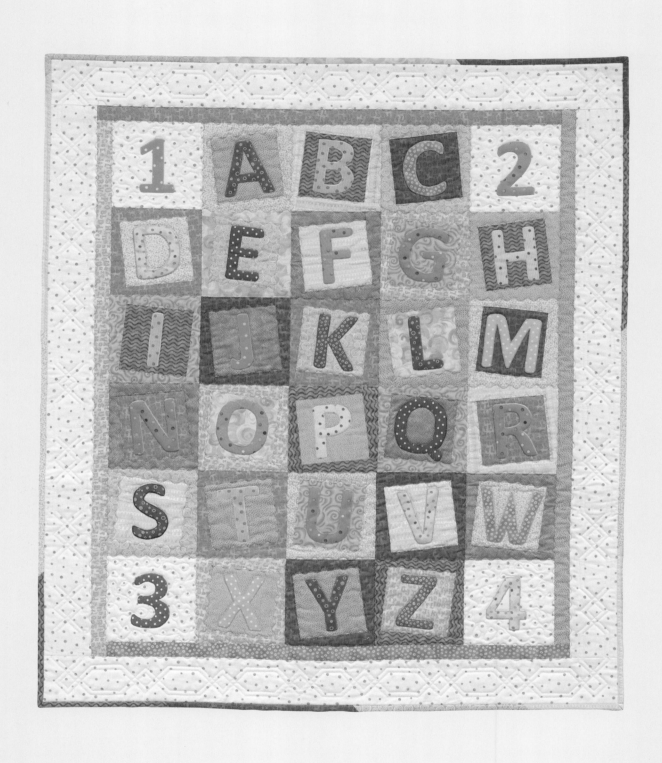

Designed, made, and machine quilted by Christine Porter

Making the Alphabet Block Backgrounds

For each block, you'll need four 2" x 7" strips cut from the same bright print.

1. Before you begin to sew, pair up a 5" blue, green, yellow, red, or orange square with a set of 2"-wide strips in a contrasting color. Make 26 sets.

2. Sewing one block at a time, and with right sides together, align the raw edges of a 2" x 7" bright-print strip with the upper-right corner and top edge of the 5" contrasting bright-print square as shown. (The opposite end of the strip will extend beyond the upper-left corner.) Sew the strip to the square, stopping approximately 2" from the upper-left corner. Press, but do not trim the strip.

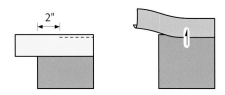

3. With right sides together, align the raw edges of a matching 2" x 7" bright-print strip with the upper-right corner and right edge of the unit from step 2. Sew the strip to the unit; press. If necessary, trim the strip even with the bottom edge of the unit.

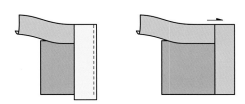

4. With right sides together, align the raw edges of a matching 2" x 7" bright-print strip with the lower-right corner and bottom edge of the unit from step 3. Sew the strip to the unit; press. If necessary, trim the strip even with the left edge of the unit.

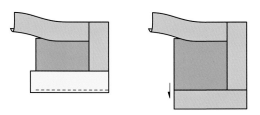

5. With right sides together, align the raw edges of the remaining matching 2" x 7" bright-print strip with the lower-left corner and left edge of the unit from step 4. Sew the strip to the unit; press. If necessary, trim the strip even with the top edge of the center square.

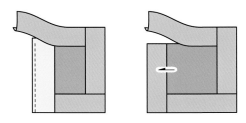

6. Complete the block by finishing the seam you started in step 2; press. If necessary, trim the top strip even with the left edge of the unit.

7. Repeat steps 2–6 to make a total of 26 background blocks.

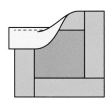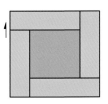

Make 26.

Trimming the Alphabet Background Blocks

1. Arrange the alphabet background blocks in a pleasing color arrangement as shown. When you're satisfied with the arrangement, you're ready to trim the blocks down to size.

2. Take the first (left) block from the top row to your cutting surface. Place a 6½" square ruler at an angle on the block, centering the 4½" marking on your ruler over the center square; trim the block to 6½" x 6½" as shown. *(Be sure to leave enough of the framing fabric for the ¼" seam allowances.)* Return the block to its proper place in the block layout.

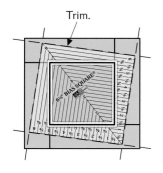

Trim.

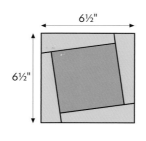

6½"

6½"

3. Skip the center block for now. Repeat step 2, tilting the ruler at the same angle to trim the last block in the row to 6½" x 6½".

4. In row 2, repeat step 2 to trim the first, third, and fifth blocks at the same angle to measure 6½" x 6½". In row 3, trim the second and fourth blocks. In row 4, trim the first, third, and fifth blocks. In row 5, trim the second and fourth blocks. In the bottom row, trim the left and right blocks.

5. Re-mark your ruler as described in "Marking Your Ruler" (opposite) so that the square is angled in the opposite direction. Trim the remaining blocks to 6½" x 6½".

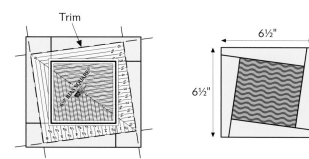

Appliquéing the Alphabet and Number Blocks

Refer to the quilt assembly diagram (opposite) and the quilt photo (page 70) for guidance in placing the appliqués.

1. Beginning with letter *A* in the top row, center the appropriate letter appliqué on each pieced background block as shown.

2. Following the manufacturer's instructions for the fusible web, adhere the appliqués to the blocks.

3. Secure the appliqués to the blocks using a machine blanket stitch or small zigzag stitch, or a hand blanket stitch.

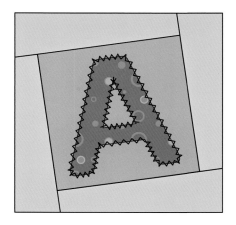

4. Repeat steps 1–3 to position, fuse, and appliqué a number to each 6½" white square. Referring to the quilt assembly diagram, place the 6½" appliquéd squares in the corners of the quilt layout.

Assembling the Quilt

1. Sew the blocks into horizontal rows; press.
2. Sew the rows together; press.

Quilt assembly

3. You'll sew the inner-border strips to this quilt using the same process that you used to sew the strips to the center of the Alphabet blocks. Refer to the quilt photo (page 70) for guidance. With right sides together, align the raw edges of the 1½" x 31½" orange strip with the upper-right corner and top edge of the quilt top. (The opposite end of the strip will extend beyond the upper-left corner.) Sew the strip to the top edge of the quilt, stopping approximately 2" from the upper-left corner. Press, but do not trim the strip.

4. With right sides together, align the raw edges of the 1½" x 37½" turquoise strip with the upper-right corner and right edge of the quilt. Sew the strip to the right edge of the quilt; press.

5. With right sides together, align the raw edges of the 1½" x 31½" green strip with the lower-right corner and bottom edge of the quilt. Sew the strip to the bottom edge of the quilt; press.

6. With right sides together, align the raw edges of the 1½" x 37½" yellow strip with the lower-left corner and left edge of the quilt. Sew the strip to the left edge of the quilt; press.

7. Complete the inner border by finishing the seam you started in step 3; press.

8. Measure the quilt through the center from top to bottom, and cut two 3¾"-wide white strips to this measurement. With right sides together, sew the strips to the sides of the quilt. Press the seam allowances toward the newly added border.

9. Measure the quilt through the center from side to side, including the borders you've just added. Cut the remaining 3¾"-wide white strips to this measurement, and sew them to the top and bottom of the quilt; press.

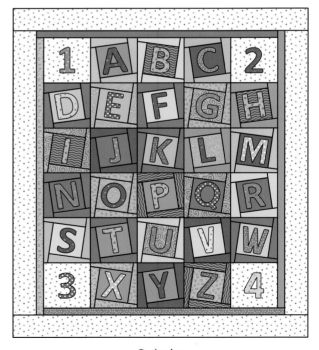

Quilt plan

Detail of quilting on "Alphabet Soup"

SUGGESTIONS FOR QUILTING

Chris used a brightly colored variegated thread to quilt wavy lines along the outside edges of the blocks, following both the vertical and horizontal seams. She then used the same thread and wavy-line motif to stitch along the edges of the center square in each Alphabet block and along the seams on both sides of the inner border.

Switching to clear monofilament, Chris closely outlined each letter and number with free-motion quilting. After stippling the backgrounds of the Number blocks with cream-colored thread, she moved to the outer border, where she used the same thread to quilt a continuous chain motif.

Finishing the Quilt

Refer to "Finishing" (page 9) as needed. For step-by-step instructions on quilt-finishing techniques (layering, basting, quilting, binding, and much more), please visit ShopMartingale.com/ HowtoQuilt.

1. Lay out the backing so the seam runs horizontally and add the batting and quilt top; baste.

2. Hand or machine quilt as desired.

3. Use the 2½"-wide assorted bright strips to finish the edges of your quilt, incorporating a label and sleeve.

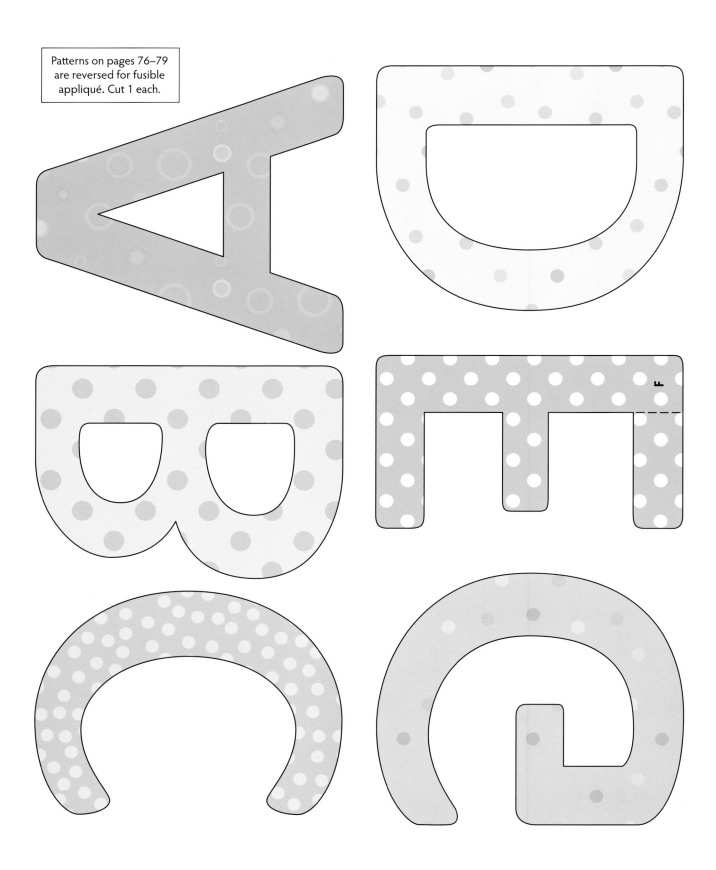

Patterns on pages 76–79 are reversed for fusible appliqué. Cut 1 each.

alphabet soup

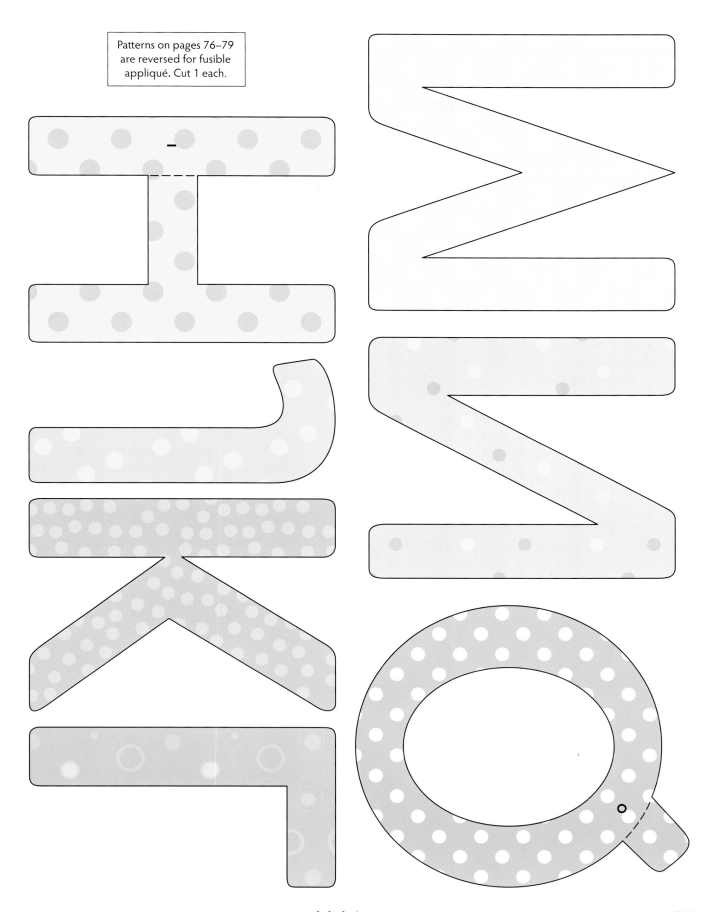

Patterns on pages 76–79 are reversed for fusible appliqué. Cut 1 each.

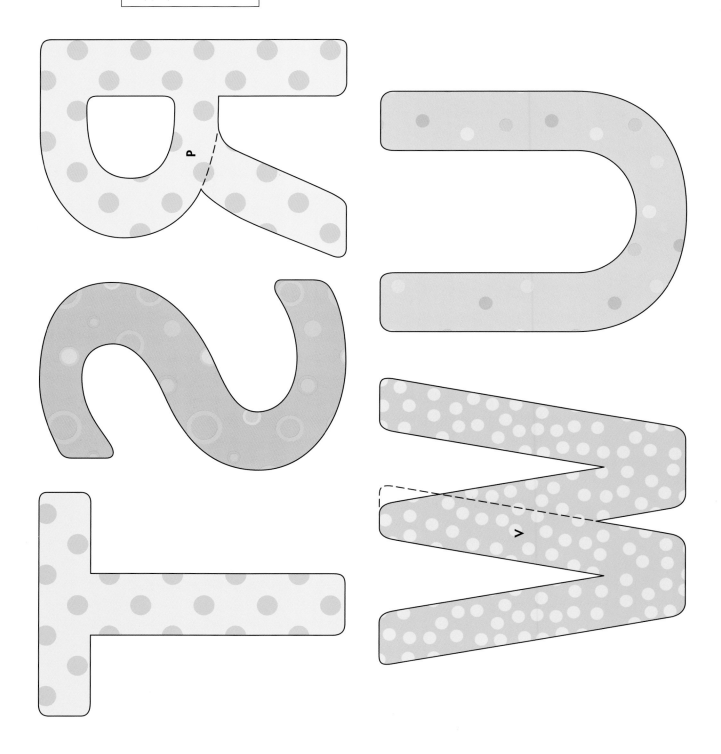

alphabet soup

Patterns on pages 76–79 are reversed for fusible appliqué. Cut 1 each.

about the authors

Darra Williamson and Christine Porter

In her 30-year career as a quilter, **Darra (Duffy) Williamson** has won awards for both her quilts and her teaching; in 1989, she was named Quilt Teacher of the Year by *Professional Quilter* magazine. She has lectured, taught, and judged for guilds and at conferences all over the United States, in the United Kingdom, and on numerous quilting cruises; written countless magazine articles and a best-selling book on scrap quilts; worked as editorial director for a major quilt-book publisher; and—as a freelancer—acquired, edited, and/or contributed to well over 100 quilting books, patterns, and other materials. Now living in the San Francisco Bay area, Darra confines her freelance work to her position as contributing editor for *The Quilt Life* magazine, choosing to focus on creating her own quilts, books, and articles, and popular blog. This is her second book for Martingale & Company.

Christine Porter has taught, lectured, and judged for guilds, and at conferences and seminars throughout Great Britain and the United States, including the International Quilt Festival in Houston, Pacific International Quilt Festival, World Quilt & Textile Show, Mid-Atlantic Quilt Festival, Empty Spools Seminars, and Road to California. She also teaches on cruises for Quilt Seminars at Sea, and has taught in Australia, Canada, Ireland, Scotland, France, Norway, New Zealand, and Dubai.

Christine sews exclusively on Husqvarna Viking sewing machines, and has won awards for her quilts in Britain and the United States. Formerly co-editor of *Patchwork & Quilting* magazine, she is now a freelance writer. She has written five books on quilting, and has made four DVDs for beginners and experienced quilters. This is also her second book for Martingale.

Visit Christine's website for information regarding her quilts, books, and classes: www.christineporterquilts.com.

Visit Darra's blog, a collaboration with three other talented quilters, authors, and teachers: www.seehowwesew.wordpress.com.